The People's History

Sunderland

'Til I Die

by

Alan Brett & Andrew Clark

Bob Moncur shoots for goal at Roker Park in the mid 1970s.

Previous page: Rebecca, Harry and Charlotte Richardson outside the Stadium of Light.

First published in 1999 by

The People's History Ltd
Suite 1
Byron House
Seaham Grange Business Park
Seaham
Co. Durham
SR7 0PY

ISBN 1 902527 07 0

Contents

Acknowledgements

Tariq Ahmed, Tracy Ahmed, Albert Anderson, Richie Ankers, Natalie Barraclough, Kevin Brady, Julie Brown, Ian Brunskill, Michael Bute, Ian S. Carr, Andrew Chapman, Ray Charlton, Dave Chester, Dave Chevington, Peter Collins, Philip Curtis, George Faller, Peter Farrer, Pearce Gibson, Fred Hagel, Ray Hassan, Neil Henderson, George Hoare, Keith Hulsmeier, Marcus Johnson, Matthew Johnson, Rachel Johnson, Andrea Lane, Bernie Lane, Michael Lane, Paul Lavelle, Kevin Lavelle, Terry Lavelle, Michael McDonagh, Ronnie McGuire, Paul Menzies, Harry Newton, Jackie O'Halloran, Andrew Pace, Jim Pace, Ray Redman, Phil Reynolds, Jeff Richardson, Dougie Smith, Michael Stephenson, Scot Stewart, Ashley Sutherland, Lily Turnbull, Tommy Turnbull, Ray Watson, Susan Wilkinson, John Yearnshire.

Special thanks to Ian Wright, Peter Martin & Derek Laidler and all at Rufus.

Bibliography

Brian Clough with John Sadler *Clough The Autobiography* Partridge Press 1994
Jimmy Greaves *This One's On Me* Arthur Barker 1979
George Hardwick *Gentleman George* Juniper Publishing 1998
Mike Kirkup *Jackie Milburn In Black And White* Stanley Paul 1990
Peter Morris *Aston Villa* The Sportsman's Book Club 1962
Ivan Sharpe *The Football League Jubilee Book* Stanley Paul 1963

Newspapers & Journals

Sunderland Echo
Football Echo
Evening Chronicle
Sunday Sun
Football Monthly
Football Evening News
Sporting Green

Introduction

Even after a record breaking promotion in 1999 few fans would have imagined the impact that Sunderland would have in the Premiership. To hold our own in the top three of the Premier, alongside Manchester United, Arsenal and Chelsea, is a new experience for many supporters who have known little else than relegation battles or years out of the top flight.

After more than two years in the Stadium of Light Sunderland fans have turned the ground into a fortress where The Lads are almost unbeatable. Roker Park will always have a special place in the hearts of every fan who witnessed a match there but now our new ground is home. Even after a little over two seasons there have already been many exciting games, outstanding performances and great goals from new heroes.

Many of the stories is this new collection from Alan Brett and Andrew Clark reflect the excitement of this new era. Starting with tales from the 'Red and White Army', the authors move on to recall favourite players, famous games and memorable away trips. The Stadium of Light's first taste of the Premiership is also featured.

In compiling this collection of stories the authors have listened to many tales of how much the club means to its supporters who will follow 'Sunderland 'Til They Die'.

Sunderland supporters at the Stadium of Light for the England international against Belgium in October 1999.

Fans' Favourites – Niall Quinn and Gary Bennett.

SECTION ONE

RED AND WHITE ARMY

The Red and White Army gather in the Howard Arms in Roker Avenue.

Paul Lavelle showing there is only one team in his life. Paul was even younger when he started following Sunderland, as a 3-year-old he used to sing along to 'Cheer up Peter Reid'.

Special Day

I was 10 years old when I went to the 1973 semi-final at Hillsborough. The streets after the game were choc-a-block with jubilant Sunderland fans. There was a wedding car inching its way through the crowd. Some Sunderland supporters got the bride out of the car to give her a wedding day kiss.

Kevin Lavelle

Lucky It Was A Girl

Shay Given is the best Sunderland goalkeeper I've seen. When he was on loan in the 1995-96 season he was absolutely brilliant. There's no doubt he helped Sunderland clinch promotion that season. My girlfriend Christine was having a baby at the time and if it was a boy we were going to call him Shay. I am pleased we had a daughter Kirsty Ann because he was on his way shortly after to Newcastle!

Michael Lane

Nicola Purvis in 1973 with her dad's Wembley hat. Nicola has a longer-lasting memento from Sunderland's Cup win. She was featured in *Sunderland Ha'Way The Lads* under her full name: Nicola Montgomery Malone Guthrie Horswill Watson Pitt Hughes Porterfield Halom Kerr Tueart Young Stokoe Purvis.

Michael and Kirsty Ann Lane.

A Sunderland 'Del Boy'

In January 1931 the *Sunderland Echo* recalled one supporter's determination to see The Lads in an FA Cup tie at Southampton despite a shortage of cash:

A Sunderland football 'fan' who is working in London at present, certainly knows his way round. He was anxious to see the cup-tie at Southampton, but found that there was no excursion from London. The fare from London to Southampton, in fact, was greater than the excursion fare from Sunderland to Southampton.

He had a brainwave. He decided to travel by the cheap 'Spurs' excursion to Portsmouth, thereby saving several shillings. On arrival at Portsmouth he spent 2s 6d on a return ticket to Southampton.

He arrived at the Southampton ground some time after the start. He saw several people who had fainted being carried out. The ground was packed by a record crowd. He walked straight through the main gates. 'Where are you going,' shouted an official. 'I'm going inside,' he replied. 'I've just been helping to carry somebody out.'

He got inside the ground and saw the game without paying. The Southampton supporters did not get any change out of him either, for during an argument with some of them he silenced them with the remark, 'They hadn't ought to allow village teams like Southampton to play in the Cup.'

Former Arsenal star Steve Bould has been inspirational since his move to the Stadium of Light.

Roker Park by the sea – the old ground in the last days of its long life. The site is now occupied by housing. Some of the street names commemorate the estate's footballing links: Promotion Close, Clockstand Close, Midfield Drive and Roker Park Close.

Supporters in The Triangle bar in Benidorm to watch the first game in the Premier against Chelsea on satellite TV. Newcastle supporters in the pub cheered when the goals went in but soon shut up when they heard Shearer was sent off against Aston Villa and they went down to defeat at St James'.

Sunderland in the Sun

When I was on holiday in Ibiza I watched two of Sunderland's Premier games live on television. In a bar in San Antonio I sat next to a Derby supporter for Sunderland's visit to Pride Park. The live pictures had a Spanish commentary but this was turned down and we tuned into Radio 5 coverage of the match. I couldn't believe it as the goals rattled in. My chest swelled out with pride as the scoreline climbed and climbed. The Derby lad was left speechless.

Near the end of the holiday I watched the Sheffield Wednesday game live, again with a supporter from the opposing team next to me. Again it was the Sunderland supporters who had something to shout about. There were a few Mags in the bar but they just kept looking over at us, I think with envy.

Dave Chester

Right: Sunderland fans on a wet day at Wembley for the 1992 FA Cup Final. Left to right: Steve Atkinson, Dave Chester, Paul Newton and Martin Nicholson.

Mike Kulik in Sunderland colours in his bedroom in Moscow. In Russia Mike is kept in touch with Sunderland's progress through George Forster of the Supporters Association.

Deaths in the Family

In the late 1970s and early '80s my brother Terry used to work the 2 pm-10 pm shift at Pyrex. If Sunderland had a mid-week match he would get me to ring him at work. The foreman would tell him there was an urgent phone call. He would then say there had been a death in the family and he got the rest of the shift off to go to the game. I'm sure the foreman knew what was happening because nobody could have had as many deaths in the family on match days as we had.

Kevin Lavelle

If You Hate Newcastle …

I remember during one derby game when the Sunderland fans started chanting 'Ha'way The Lads' the Newcastle supporters gave us a round of mock applause. Later a Newcastle fan told me that Sunderland fans shouldn't chant 'Ha'way The Lads' – it was their battle cry. What rubbish! No wonder we hate them.

Ronnie McGuire

Kings of Northumberland

It's remarkable how Northumberland continues to have a soft spot for Sunderland – excluding of course, Newcastle itself … a big section of the community in Northumberland, even as far as Rothbury, favour Sunderland … The explanation of that is that Sunderland were in the early days the only first-class club in the district, and the Sunderland tradition has been carried on through generations.

Football Echo, 26th January 1935

Sunderland Is The Drug

I was taken to my first Sunderland match by my dad in 1955. The game was against Cardiff City and when we got in I was passed over the heads of people down to the touchline. I started to panic and shouted 'Da, Da, what's happening?' I didn't know this was how youngsters were placed in safe areas. I was 12 years old at the time and I've been addicted ever since.

Matty Morrison

Right: Norman Wisdom on a visit to Roker Park. Some supporters would say he wasn't the only comedian to appear at the old stadium.

The packed Fulwell End terracing at Roker Park. All-seater stadia have allowed parents to feel safe to have their children at football matches. A large part of the Stadium of Light is taken up by families with young children.

World Cup 2006 & 1966

The announcement that Sunderland forms a crucial part of England's bid for the 2006 World Cup is terrific news for the club and the city. In October 1999 a FIFA delegation inspected the Stadium of Light. World Cup hat-trick hero Geoff Hurst accompanied the party on the tour of the stadium. If England's bid is successful Sunderland is lined up as a semi-final venue by which time the ground's capacity would be over sixty thousand.

Sunderland Council Leader, Colin Anderson, reported that the delegation were impressed with Sunderland. He said: 'I was at Roker Park for World Cup football in 1966 and I hope to be at the Stadium of Light for World Cup football in 2006.'

The world's best in action at Roker Park in 1966. Lev Yashin (USSR) claims the ball from Florian Albert (Hungary) in a quarter-final clash.

Right: An advert from October 1966 for *Goal* – the film of the 1966 World Cup. The *Echo* reviewed the film: 'Remember the brilliant Eusebio in tears after Portugal's semi-final defeat by England? Or the Russian goalkeeper, Lev Yashin, swooping apparently from the sky at Roker to clutch safely like 'Batman' as he was styled by Wearsider supporters?'

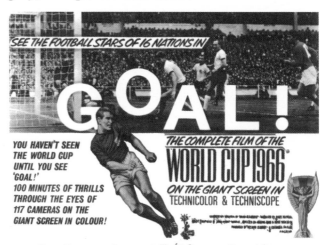

World Cup here we come! When the Stadium of Light staged England's international against Belgium in October 1999 it could be a taste of things to come if the 2006 World Cup comes to this country. The Stadium of Light is already being talked about as a venue for a semi-final game.

Sunderland exile Ray Hassan.

Derby Tension

I live in Surrey and so it is difficult to follow Sunderland's fortunes. You almost feel helpless because you are so far away from The Lads. When we played Newcastle this season I switched on teletext to see the Mags had taken the lead. Then later when we equalised I would have been happy to settle for a draw. I was panicking now – hoping we could just hang on. When we took the lead I couldn't take it any more. I switched off the television and went to the bottom of the garden – the tension was so great. I just paced up and down waiting for the final whistle. I came back into the house to be told we had claimed a great victory.

Ray Hassan

The New Shirt

A couple of weeks before the 1992 FA Cup Final with Liverpool, I posted a cheque to Sunderland AFC, to buy the season's away shirt. I'd been meaning to buy the shirt for ages, and it had just been announced that Liverpool would be playing in their home colours, so Sunderland would wear that particular shirt in the Final. I thought it would be nice if it arrived in time, so that I could wear my new shirt to Wembley.

A few days before the big day, my new shirt arrived in the post. It was the white one, with the green and blue flash on the shoulders. I opened the package and held up the shirt. Brilliant, I thought, that'll look great on Saturday. I whipped off my t-shirt and tried the new shirt on. As I was admiring myself in the dining room mirror, I noticed one of the family cats sitting on the table. I turned to stroke her and, messing around, asked her if she liked my new kit. She took this acknowledgement as a signal to jump up into my arms, dragging her back claws across my new white shirt as she did so. I couldn't believe it. There was a huge line of pulled threads, right across the front under the VAUX logo. A few moments earlier I was imagining myself at Wembley, looking my best, and cheering on The Lads. Now I was looking down at my ruined shirt. It had only been out of the packaging thirty seconds. I could have cried. And yes, she IS a black cat too!

Neil Henderson

Neil and Karen Henderson at the Stadium of Light, August 1999.

From The Promised Land To Disney Land

My first football match was Gordon Armstrong's testimonial match against Porto at Roker Park when I was 5 years old. I got a season ticket when the Stadium of Light opened. The best match I have ever been to was Birmingham City when we won promotion. The best goal I have seen was Kevin Phillips

strike against Barnsley. Super Kev is my favourite player. The best laugh I had was when Niall Quinn was dancing and doing impressions behind an Ipswich defender's back.

In May 1999 I went to Euro Disney on holiday. The best part of my holiday was watching Newcastle get beat in the FA Cup Final, even though it was in French.

Andrew Chapman

Andrew Chapman with his Uncle Terry (right).

A New Experience

When I went to Kevin Ball's testimonial it was my first football match at the age of 85. I really enjoyed the experience. The Stadium of Light was very impressive and we had a wonderful view of the game. It reminded me of a bull ring in Spain. I had been around the old stadium at Roker Park on a tour and while that was cosy the new ground is big and bright.

Lily Turnbull

Right: Kevin Ball has always given 100% commitment to the Sunderland cause. Italian club Sampdoria provided the opposition for his testimonial in July 1999.

Vaux Breweries

Sunderland 'Til They Died

When the gates of Vaux Breweries closed for the last time in July 1999 it marked the end of a Sunderland institution. When Sunderland AFC was founded in 1879, Vaux had been going for 42 years as a company.

Cuthbert Vaux worked in a brewery in Low Street in the East End in the early part of the nineteenth century. In the 1830s he left to go into partnership with William Story in Union Street. After the partnership ended a new company was formed and Vaux went on to become a household name in Sunderland right up to the present day.

The Brewery had a long association with the club with beer like Maxim Ale and Double Maxim being advertised in match programmes between the wars. This continued with brands like Lorimer, Norseman, Samson and Lambtons appearing in programmes since the war.

In the mid-1980s shirt sponsorship began and continued right up to its closure. The Lambton logo graced the Sunderland shirts as promotion to the Premiership was achieved at the end of the 1998-99 season. This was to prove the final season of not only Vaux sponsorship but of the company itself.

Over the years Vaux had been a good friend of publications like the *Sunderland Annual*, *A Love Supreme* and *The Wearside Roar*.

Above: Vaux specially brewed lager to celebrate promotion to the Premiership in 1996 and 1999.

Left: One of many Vaux adverts which appeared in Sunderland books and programmes over the years. Whatever division Sunderland were in Vaux were there with their support.

Staff at Hills Bookshop in Sunderland before the 1992 FA Cup Final.

New Found Friends

I've become great friends with the people who I sit near to at the Stadium of Light. It's as if we have known each other for years but I only met them a couple of seasons ago. I suppose we do share a common bond.

Tariq Ahmed

A family at the Stadium of Light.

Sunderland 'Til I Almost Die

I was outside the Roker End when the gates collapsed at the Manchester United game in 1964. I heard cracking noises as they started to give. My younger brother Jimmy was up a lamp-post at the time trying to get over the wall. I started to tug at his leg to warn him when the gates went crashing down. We then started to run in but just inside I tripped and was sent sprawling on the ground. In a flash my brother grabbed me and dragged me to my feet or I would have been crushed to death in the stampede to get in. We ended up on the pitch near the corner of the Roker End and Main Stand and watched the game in relative safety.

Matty Morrison

Felling Fans

I was born and brought up in Felling when almost everyone living there were black and white. Our house was football daft, my dad's Scottish and he named me after Scot Symon the Celtic and Scotland player. Along with me, there was my elder brother Gorman, and a couple of other lads who followed Sunderland. I saw my first game at Roker Park when I was eight. The match was against Swindon Town on 3rd April 1971. I stood in the Roker End with Gorman and we won 5-2. A week later I went to my first away match. It was at Middlesbrough and we drew 2-2 with goals from Billy Hughes and Dave Watson playing at centre forward.

Scot Stewart

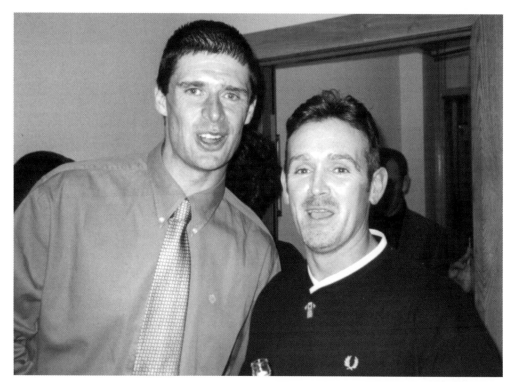

Niall Quinn with Scot Stewart after the last League match of the 1998-99 season. The big Irishman's goal in the 2-1 win over Birmingham proved costly for Scot. With a dozen games remaining he estimated Sunderland would reach 103 points. A draw against Birmingham looked on the cards, and would have meant a big payout from the bookies, until Niall popped up with the winner to give Sunderland 105 points.

Anything To Declare

Whenever I go to Newcastle Airport for holiday flights I wear my Sunderland shirt. I always seem to be picked out by customs for a suitcase search. This happened when I was jetting off to Turkey. I asked the man conducting the search what he was looking for. He replied 'Drugs.' I said 'Drugs to Turkey, isn't that like Coals to Newcastle.'

Dougie Smith

SECTION TWO

A GAME TO REMEMBER

AND A FEW TO FORGET

The official programme from the 1913 FA Cup Final at Crystal Palace.

Sunderland 0 Aston Villa 1
FA Cup Final 19th April 1913
at Crystal Palace, Attendance 120,081

Thousands of Sunderland fans poured into London for the club's first ever FA Cup Final appearance. The *Echo's* representative reported: 'One band of Sunderland supporters looked conspicuous in the Strand on top of an old English coach … Street hawkers did a roaring trade with the sale of the Villa and Sunderland club colour rosettes, and there was much good-natured humour when the partisans of both clubs got wedged in the crowd.'

A record crowd of over 120,000 packed the Crystal Palace ground to see the top two clubs in the League battle for the Cup. Villa ran out 1-0 and Sunderland had to content themselves with the League championship a few days later.

Above: The *Football Evening News* on the day of Sunderland's first FA Cup Final appearance in 1913.

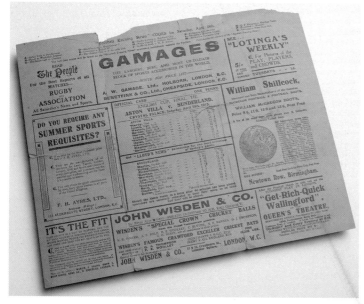

Left: The reverse of the 1913 Cup Final programme shown on the previous page.

Sunderland 2 Arsenal 1
10th April 1926 at Roker Park, Attendance 20,000

When Charlie Buchan returned to Roker Park for the first time after his transfer to Arsenal he was given a rousing reception. He led out an Arsenal team that was challenging for the title.

After 25 minutes the Gunners' championship aspirations were given a boost with a goal from centre forward Jimmy Brain. Bobby Gurney, who had been injured after only a few minutes play, got Sunderland's equaliser.

Midway through the second half, with the score still level, the referee sensationally sent off the Arsenal 'keeper Dan Lewis and Sunderland centre forward Dave Halliday. Argus in the *Sunderland Echo* reported: 'The incident was quite clear to me, and I have no hesitation in declaring that the Arsenal man was responsible for the incident. He got his leg fastened round Halliday's, and naturally Halliday, in freeing himself, hooked his leg away, and the Arsenal goalkeeper went on his back behind the touch line. In an instant he was up and attacked Halliday from behind when the Sunderland centre forward was walking away. Halliday turned and retaliated, as any man would do after being struck, and the referee promptly ordered both men to the dressing-room.'

Arsenal had to put Joe Hulme, an outfield player, in goal. A few minutes from time Bobby Gurney beat the makeshift 'keeper to give Sunderland victory.

The final incident in an eventful game was when Charlie Buchan was booed by the crowd. The former Roker idol aroused the wrath of the home supporters when he fouled Sunderland skipper Charlie Parker from behind.

A year after his sending off, Dan Lewis was involved in another controversial incident. Playing against Cardiff City in the FA Cup Final he allowed a simple shot to slip from his grasp and roll into the goal. His mistake allowed the FA Cup to leave England for the only time.

Dave Halliday ended the 1925-26 season, his first at Sunderland, with 38 goals from 42 League games. He was the top scorer at the club in each of the following three seasons before being transferred to Arsenal for a £6,500 fee. His stay at Highbury was to prove brief and he was soon on his way to Manchester City. The former Sunderland favourite made an explosive return to Roker Park with his new club on 2nd January 1932. He scored a hat-trick in eight minutes as City ran out 5-2 winners.

Dave Halliday. Former Sunderland chairman Fred Taylor was convinced Halliday was the innocent party as he shook the player's hand as he walked off the field.

Dan Lewis, Arsenal and Wales goalkeeper. Lewis went into the Sunderland dressing-room after the match to apologise to Halliday for having lost his temper.

Everton 6 Sunderland 4

30th January 1935 at Goodison Park, Attendance 59,212
FA Cup 4th Round Replay

The Blue half of Merseyside provided the opposition in one of the most thrilling FA Cup ties in FA Cup history. Everton had gained a 1-1 draw at Roker Park in a fourth round tie on 26th January 1935 and almost 60,000 people gathered at Goodison for the replay four days later. Everton were skippered by the legendary Dixie Dean.

Left winger Jack Coulter found the net twice early in the replay to give the home side a 2-0 lead. Bert Davis pulled a goal back for Sunderland five minutes before the interval. In the second half Alex Stevenson made it 3-1 but Jimmy Connor reduced the deficit to one goal. With time running out Bobby Gurney kicked the ball over his head from an almost impossible angle and it found the net for the equaliser.

At the end of ninety minutes Sunderland manager Johnny Cochrane ran on the pitch to talk to his players. The referee then got two policemen to eject him from the playing area.

Within three minutes of the start of extra time Coulter completed his hat-trick. Sunderland would still not lie down and drew level with Connor's second goal of the game. Gurney had a glorious chance to score but passed to Carter to put the ball in the net. The referee disallowed the goal for Carter being offside. Everton right winger Albert Geldard then scored twice to give the home side a stunning 6-4 victory.

Everton's Dixie Dean – The great centre forward failed to get on the scoresheet in the classic Cup tie with Sunderland.

Sunderland's Scottish international left winger Jimmy Connor scored twice at Goodison Park.

Everton's Irish international left winger Jack Coulter went one better with a hat-trick to help his side to victory.

Large crowds gathered around the Echo Office in Bridge Street and around Mackie's Corner awaiting news of the game. The police had to be called to ensure traffic could flow.

If Sunderland had overcome Everton they would have faced Derby County at home in the next round. Only two years before the Rams had been the opponents in another Cup tie when the Roker Park record attendance of 75,118 was set.

Wonder Goal

The best goal I've ever seen at Sunderland was scored by centre half Ray Daniel. It came in an FA Cup replay against Sheffield United at Roker Park in 1956. Daniel was in his own half when he got the ball and he hit a rocket shot into the goal smashing against the iron net support. Sheffield 'keeper Ted Burgin was diving when the ball was coming out.

Pearce Gibson

Despite being beaten by Daniel's long range winner, Burgin had a brilliant game in the United goal. Sheffield United boss Joe Mercer, later Manchester City and England manager, described Daniel's goal as the best he had ever seen.

DANIEL SUPPLIED RAY OF SUNSHINE

SUNDERLAND FORWARDS TRIED EVERY TRICK IN THE BOOK TO SCORE AGAINST SHEFFIELD YESTERDAY! BILL HOLDEN WAITED VAINLY FOR HIS TROOPS ONCE —

NOW FOR ME SECOND GOAL FOR 'EM!

— THEN DECIDED TO HAVE A BASH ON HIS OWN. — WITHOUT SUCCESS.

SHACK GOT SO MIXED UP WITH A CORNER FLAG — I WASN'T QUITE SURE WHETHER HE INTENDED TO — PLANT IT — OR SCORE WITH IT!

AND I'M SORRY 'LEGS' — BUT APART FROM TWO SHOTS — YOU JUST MADE A PROPER 'CHARLIE' OF YOURSELF!

WHILE BILL ELLIOTT MUST HAVE THOUGHT THE WAY TO GET A GOAL AT ONE TIME WAS TO KNEEL DOWN AND FACE MECCA!

IT WAS LEFT TO RAY DANIEL TO SCORE FROM SO FAR OUT — HE MUST HAVE USED RADAR TO FIND THE NET!

The *Echo's* view of Sheffield United's FA Cup visit to Roker Park in 1956.

It Doesn't Rain But It Pours

I'll never forget Sunderland's semi-final against Manchester City in 1955. I went with my brother-in-law Harry Newton. We went for a drink around the town on the Friday night and then boarded the coach at the Plaza. The coach had to plough through water on the roads on the journey down. It poured down in Birmingham. I bought a corduroy cap to keep the rain off but by half time this had shrunk. The pitch was a quagmire. I can picture today, George Aitken kicking a ball that went like a ship through the water on the pitch. Manchester City won 1-0 and denied Sunderland a Wembley clash with Newcastle. After the game we went in a pub in the Bull Ring to dry out. We had pints and whiskies while our clothes dried in front of the fire.

George Faller

A Century Of Rivalry

Sunderland vs Newcastle United

The uproar aroused by the Lee Clark T shirt affair shows the depth of feeling between the Sunderland-Newcastle United rivalry.

Since the first League derby in 1898 there have been some titanic battles to see who would claim to be the top team in the North East.

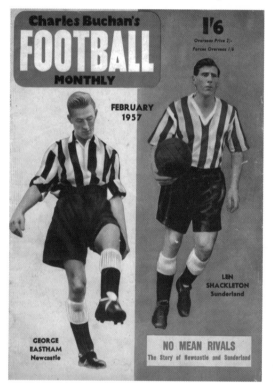

Gary, Gabby & Gatesy

The Sunderland matches I remember best were both at Newcastle. I was there when Gary Rowell scored his hat-trick in the 4-1 win. Gary and his Sunderland team-mates were just irresistible that day.

I couldn't get in for the Play-off semi-final so we went in the pubs outside St James' Park. We listened to the commentary trying hard not to reveal our allegiances. We had to order our drinks in Tyneside accents. Goals from Marco Gabbiadini and Eric Gates put us through to the Final. Even a pitch invasion by Newcastle supporters could not change the result. 4-1 and 2-0 in their own backyard, brilliant.

Dougie Smith

Left: The cover of the *Football Monthly* in February 1957.

The Day Newcastle United Almost Went On Strike

The time Sunderland's Len Shackleton almost got the Newcastle players to boycott the 1951 FA Cup Final was revealed in Mike Kirkup's book *Jackie Milburn In Black And White*. Jackie Milburn recalled:

That's why I came to admire Shack more than anybody. He insisted that we were playing for buttons. He insisted on this, way back to the war years. Aye! In fact, he came over just before the '51 Final – he was playing for Sunderland at the time – and spoke to the lads. 'Hey, you want to refuse to go on the bloody pitch,' he says, 'because they're making nearly forty thousand pounds on the gate'.

It was three and a tanner for a ticket then, and about a couple of quid for a seat, or something. And he went through the whole routine of what they were clicking, the FA, and how much they were making, and what we were getting.

The Newcastle team did not take Shack's advice because they feared if they refused to play the board would have drafted in 11 reserves for the Final!

INCIDENTS IN THE GREAT GAME AT GALLOWGATE. THE "SUNDAY SUN" ARTIST ILLUSTRATES POINTS IN THE STRUGGLE.

How the *Sunday Sun* saw Sunderland's League visit to St James' on 29th November 1919. Goals from Barney Travers (2) and Jackie Mordue helped Sunderland to a 3-2 victory before a crowd of 61,761. A week before Sunderland had completed the first leg of a double over their old rivals at Roker Park. A brace of goals from Charlie Buchan gave Sunderland maximum points in the first post-war derby.

A Warm Welcome

When Newcastle won the Cup in 1951 the team stopped off at Sunderland Railway Station on the way home. Thousands in and around the station gave the players a rousing reception. There was a deafening roar as the crowd spotted Jackie Milburn. It's hard to imagine something like that happening today.

Albert Anderson

Whistle Stop Visit

The train carrying the Newcastle United players pulled into Sunderland Station at 6.12 on the evening of 3rd May 1951 and departed three minutes later. Jackie Milburn said he would have liked to have stopped off to give the people of Sunderland a good look at the cup. But they wanted to get home after being away for a fortnight.

Newcastle United 1

St James' Park

When some beardless boys have become grandfathers they will gather the younger generation round them and tell a tale of Tyneside, about eleven stalwart Sunderland footballers who travelled to St James' Park and thrashed the famous Novocastrians as if they had been a poor lot of unfortunates from some home for the blind. The greatest match of this season in the North provided the sensation of the year, and we shall have to turn back to the days when the game was in its infancy for a parallel performance in a match reputedly of high class.

This was 'the majority match' of the redoubtable rivals of the North East coast. I mean that it was their 21st in connection with the League tournament, and the wicked Wearside wreckers besmirched the 'scutcheon of Newcastle with a big blot that cannot be obliterated, even by Time, the great healer of wounds, Sunderland established a record in this match.

Goal was piled on goal in the second half until the Geordies must have been sick at heart. To properly appreciate the collapse of Newcastle let me say that, though the teams were on an equality at the interval, the Wearside cohorts swooped down on the Tyneside fold with such irresistible rushes that they scored eight goals in 28 minutes during one period of the second half ... Newcastle United, like most clubs which have made history, have befallen some strange experiences, but their last is in some senses the most extraordinary and the most humiliating.

The game was only eight minutes old when Hogg dashed ahead, and Lawrence, realizing that he was uncovered, went to meet his man. He and Hogg seemed to be on the ball at the same time, but the Sunderland captain got in his shot as Lawrence fell, and the ball slowly rolled into a tenantless goal ...

The visitors played so well that the United defence were seldom given a rest. However, a minute before half-time the referee awarded a penalty kick for hands by Thomson ... Shepherd netting with a high drive. Thus was the record made level ...

The Wearsiders overwhelmed their opponents (in the second half). They threaded their way through them as easily as the circus rider jumps through the tissue-paper hoops (Holley 3, Hogg and Bridgett each 2, and Mordue increasing the score).

James Lawrence, the Newcastle United goalkeeper who was beaten nine times by the rampaging Sunderland side.

Sunderland 9

5th December 1908

All these goals had been, as said, notched in 28 minutes, and the last five of them in eight minutes. The Sunderland forwards simply lined up in procession time after time, left their opponents floundering in the roar, and bombarded and shelled the goal as easily as they would light a cigarette. And Holley's smile would have made the Goddess of Tragedy laugh.

Such is an outline sketch of a memorable match, the like of which we may not see for years. Sunderland were far the heavier team, and they suffered the grey scene and the dark surroundings with their dare-devil dash ... but Arthur Brown rather reminded me of the boy who sat in the tree while the giant carried it along, and then when they had arrived the boy glided off the branch and said: 'We've done it' ... Holley was the deftest and most dangerous forward on the field. His shooting is proverbial, and I question if England ever was so blessed with inside-lefts, for there are at least three men worthy of a cap, and Holley is one of them ...

The half-backs were a dour set, with one outstanding figure, and he Charlie Thomson. The man is a host, and so robust that he needs either a very powerful man or a very cunning centre to outwit him. Shepherd has the strength, but not the craft ...

I should like to say something to comfort Newcastle United in their hour of trouble, but there are few crumbs of consolation to be discovered, I do not blame Lawrence. The poor man was there to be shot at, as he had not any cover or protection from the backs ... Both backs made the dreadful mistake of placing the ball at the toes of Sunderland forwards. This was like trying to keep back the tide with a besom ... Veitch was the one man who showed solidity and class, but what is one among so many? The team, as a whole, had neither the physique nor experience to cope with such opponents. If nine tailors make a man, what do nine goals make? Ask Newcastle.

Newcastle United: Lawrence; Whitson, Pudan; Liddell, Veitch, Willis; Duncan, Higgins, Shepherd, Wilson and Gosnell.

Sunderland: L.R. Roose; Forster, Milton; Low, Thomson, Daykin; Mordue, Hogg, Brown, Holley and Bridgett.

Tityrus
Athletic News,
7th December 1908

Black Cats – Top Dogs

Journalist Frank Lonsdale was at the victory at St James' Park in 1908. He recounted how the 'Black Cat Killed The Magpie' on that famous day: 'The Wearside fans that night celebrated until the early hours. And many there were who had one over the eight – to match their team's score!'

Newcastle United 1 Sunderland 2

25th August 1999 at St James' Park, Attendance 36,600

In the long history of Sunderland-Newcastle United derbies there has surely never been a game played in such conditions. Downpours before and during the game made the pitch treacherous for both sides with surface water getting deeper as the match progressed.

The major talking point before a ball had been kicked was Sunderland-born Paul Robinson being preferred to England captain Alan Shearer in the United line-up. Ruud Guillit's decision appeared to be justified when Robinson set up Kieron Dyer to put Newcastle ahead in the 28th minute. The goal came against the run of play as Sunderland had made the early going.

Midway through the second half Nicky Summerbee's cross was met perfectly by Niall Quinn who sent a glancing header past 'keeper Tommy Wright for the equaliser. Ten minutes later man of the match Summerbee found Kevin Phillips in space and the little striker scored with a brilliant chip after having his first attempt saved by Wright.

There was a heart-stopping moment at the end when Kevin Ball's challenge sent the ball soaring over Tommy Sorenson but the ball hit the bar. This narrow escape confirmed it was to be Sunderland's night.

The national press and the *Match of the Day* coverage centred on Guillit's decision to drop Shearer. They did not give Sunderland the credit they deserved in coming back from 1-0 down to record a superb victory.

As well as the 800 Sunderland supporters at St James' Park a further 16,000 watched a beam back of the match at the Stadium of Light. An unforgettable night for Sunderland supporters everywhere.

The Day After

I went into Sunderland Library the day after Sunderland's 2-1 win at St James' to read all the newspaper coverage of the game. The headlines read 'Gullit's gamble backfires' and 'Gullit on the brink'. All the papers blamed Newcastle's defeat on the dropping of Shearer. The national press did not give Sunderland the credit they deserved for a fantastic victory. As Gullit said afterwards they were winning 1-0 before Ferguson and Shearer got on the field. As we were reading the papers a lad of about sixteen came over and asked how Sunderland got on. An old guy said with amazement they won 2-1. 'Oh, great' the lad said, then went off. A man at the next table said, 'Where's he been?' The old man replied, 'He must have been on another planet.'

Tommy Taylor

Newcastle Nurse

I was in hospital the night of the Newcastle game. I had a very bad infection so had a private room with a television. When highlights of the game were on TV a couple of nurses came into my room to watch it. One of them was a Newcastle fan and she was very quiet. Then she turned to me and joked, 'Watch what you say I've got to look after you for the next twelve hours.'

Tracy Ahmed

Singing In The Rain

As my dad and I were walking home after watching the beam back at the Stadium of Light we saw some funny scenes. People were dancing about as the rain poured down. There was a building with a drain pipe broken off with water gushing down about 12 feet from the ground. One lad just stood under and got a 'shower'.

Rachel Johnson

Jimmy Montgomery and Cecil Irwin deny Newcastle's Wyn Davies a chance on goal in the match at St James' on 29th October 1966. Sunderland pulled off a great 3-0 win against their old rivals.

Goalmouth action from the derby clash at Roker Park on 8th April 1977. Goals from Kevin Arnott and Bob Lee gave Sunderland a share of the points in a 2-2 draw.

Revie Plan

The first Sunderland game I ever went to at Roker Park was against Manchester City on Good Friday 1956. Don Revie was the key player at City at the time. The famous 'Revie Plan' was based on the Hungarian Nandor Hideguti's deep-lying centre forward role which had destroyed England in 1953. From the kick off Revie passed the ball to the wing and from a cross George Aitken scored in his own goal to give the visitors the lead after less than a minute's play. Revie completed a 3-0 victory for City when he scored two minutes from the end. The following season he joined Sunderland but could not repeat the success he enjoyed with the Manchester club.

Michael Bute

Sunderland skipper Don Revie with Leeds United's John Charles at Elland Road. After leaving Sunderland for Leeds in 1958 he built up the Yorkshire club into one of the finest in Europe.

Mass Hysteria

I arrived at Roker Park at about 5 o'clock for the FA Cup replay against Manchester United in 1964. We started to queue for the Roker End and when the turnstiles opened the queues were orderly. Then at around 6 o'clock panic seemed to set in with people fearing they would not get in. The queues merged into a mass of people. I was about ten yards from the turnstile when it closed. Nearby the big double gates gave way and hundreds got in. There must have been 100,000 people trying to get in the ground that night. We stood around outside until half time and then made our way home. It was a frightening experience.

Ray Charlton

Unbelievable

The FA Cup replay against Manchester City in 1973 was the best game I've ever been to. The atmosphere was absolutely electric that night and to beat a side with stars like Francis Lee, Colin Bell and Rodney Marsh was unbelievable. The 'buzz' at that match was even better than the Final.

Dave Chester

Sunderland 1 Aston Villa 3
12th January 1963 at Roker Park, Attendance 33,237
League Cup Semi-Final (First Leg)

A record League Cup gate of 33,237 gathered at Roker Park to see if Sunderland could take a healthy lead to Birmingham for the second leg. The pitch and terracing were covered in snow and the match was one of only four out of 46 English games to go ahead on that Saturday afternoon.

Villa adapted to the difficult conditions better in the first half and took a 2-0 lead through Crowe and Thomson. After the interval Nicky Sharkey pulled a goal back for Sunderland. Midway through the half Jimmy Montgomery was injured and though he continued, eventually had to leave the field. Full back Colin Nelson took over in goal and with the Roker Roar behind them ten-man Sunderland went in search of the equaliser. Despite putting the Villa goal under pressure for the last 20 minutes of the match they could not breakthrough. Just before the end the visitors got a third goal through Derek Dougan, who was later to have a long career with Wolves.

The return leg at Villa Park ended 0-0 and Aston Villa progressed to the Final where they were beaten by local rivals Birmingham City. Sunderland had to wait another 22 years before they reached a League Cup Final.

Action from Sunderland's League match with Sheffield United on Guy Fawkes' Day 1966. Jim Baxter inspired Sunderland to a 4-1 victory. The stylish Scot got one of the goals with Neil Martin (2) and Gary Moore completing the scoring.

Teesside Memories

Sunderland vs Middlesbrough

Action from a Wear-Tees derby from after the Second World War, in the days when 50,000 crowds were common place at Roker Park. Note the standing supporters in the second tier of the Main Stand before seats were installed in 1950.

Gordon Armstrong wins a heading duel against Middlesbrough at Ayresome Park in 1990.

Ian Porterfield hits the post with Middlesbrough 'keeper Jim Platt well beaten while Graeme Souness (4) and Bryan Robson (10) look on. The match at Ayresome Park on 2nd August 1975 was part of the Anglo-Scottish pre-season competition. The Teessiders ran out 3-2 winners.

Middlesbrough's Paul Gascoigne gets a warm welcome from a Sunderland supporter.

Stoke City 0 Sunderland 0
FA Cup 5th Round 14th February 1976
Victoria Ground, Attendance 41,176

Bobby Moncur in a heading duel with Ian Moores. There was no loved lost in this St Valentine's Day clash at Stoke as the sides fought out a goalless draw.

Stoke City were in the top flight at the time and had stars like Peter Shilton (pictured), Alan Hudson, Jimmy Greenhoff and Terry Conroy in the side.

Sunderland 2 Stoke City 1
FA Cup 5th Round Replay 17th February 1976
Roker Park, Attendance 47,583

Future Sunderland manager Denis Smith watches Peter Shilton safely gather the ball in the replay at Roker.

Mel Holden is mobbed by his team-mates after giving Sunderland the lead after 75 minutes play. Denis Smith snatched a Stoke equaliser before Bryan Robson ensured victory ten minutes from the end. This set up a quarter final tie at Roker against Crystal Palace which Sunderland lost 1-0.

In A League Of Their Own
By Andrea Lane

The journey from Roker Park to our fabulous new footballing arena was an emotional one for all of those connected with the football club. What occurred between our concluding competitive match at Roker and our opening encounter at the Stadium of Light was heartbreaking for supporters, players and management alike. The club was relegated from the Premier League.

May 3rd, 1997 will go down as a historic day in the annals of Sunderland AFC. It was the final time in the ground's ninety-nine-year existence, that The Lads would grace the hallowed turf, at the traditional time of three o'clock on a Saturday afternoon. It was a fitting tribute to the ground and all those who had ever inhabited it, that the team put on a fantastic display and totally outclassed their Merseyside opponents.

Sunderland entered the game not knowing their fate, however, they knew that three points against Everton would go a long way towards securing their Premiership safety. The Red and White Faithful were also aware of this and for ninety minutes they did everything within their power to inspire the Rokermen. From the moment the players took to the field the famous Roker Roar could be heard from every corner of the ground. On that momentous day, each and every Sunderland fan wholeheartedly expressed their support for the team and they endured every possible emotion. The Roker Roar that afternoon must have had an inspirational effect as Sunderland ran out comfortable 3-0 winners. Paul Stewart, Chris Waddle and Allan Johnston were the men who grabbed the goals. It was particularly pleasing to see Chris Waddle send a free kick into the back of the net, in front of the packed Fulwell End. As a youngster he had stood on the terraces, consequently it provided a joyous moment for all Sunderland fans to see a fellow fan score such a cracking goal on such an important occasion.

The last League game at Roker Park – An emotional occasion for both players and supporters.

Sunderland fans are renowned for their knowledge of the game and great affinity with the team and it was the immense support of the fans which made Roker Park a truly special place. As the final whistle blew and the curtain came down on one of football's finest old stadiums, everyone of those fans took time to remember the ground and all its glories. Every single supporter had their own individual memories of games, players and people at Roker, and for a few brief minutes the home supporters recalled them. As I walked down the steps of the Fulwell End for the final time I thought that it was a tragedy that the ground wouldn't be allowed the opportunity to celebrate its centenary year. However, I was also looking forward to the prospect of watching football in a stadium which could house over forty thousand fans. I wondered if the new stadium could be as special as Roker Park, whether the answer was yes or no, Roker Park would never be forgotten.

I need never have worried about whether our new home would be special. As soon as I saw it dominating the Sunderland skyline and enhancing the banks of the River Wear I knew that it would surpass all of my greatest expectations.

Our League campaign at the Stadium of Light began with the visit of Manchester City. We badly needed a win to kick-start our season and to ensure that the dawn of a new era had a fairy tale beginning. We eventually obtained the win after participating in a game which was packed with incident. Sunderland took the lead when Niall Quinn intercepted a backpass and calmly rounded the keeper. The game was still finely balanced until City had a man sent off. However, despite their numerical disadvantage, Man City still managed to find an equaliser via the penalty spot. The goal only served as a catalyst in aiding a Sunderland victory. Summer signings, Kevin Phillips and Lee Clark produced two goals which sent the near forty thousand crowd home happy.

The atmosphere, as it had been during the final game at Roker Park, was electric and from that day forward the volume of the crowd began to intensify. Since the opening game at the Stadium of Light there have been many memorable matches. The stadium is in a different league to the vast majority of grounds in Britain. To the people of Sunderland it is more than just a football ground, it is a focal point for an entire city and this is what elevates it. To return to Roker Park would feel like taking a step back in time. Therefore to compare the two grounds would be difficult, however, each has its own distinctive qualities and each will be remembered as hugely special places in the heart of every Sunderland fan.

Off to a winning start at the Stadium of Light against Manchester City.

Chelsea 4 Sunderland 0
7th August 1999 at Stamford Bridge, Attendance 34,831

The Chelsea team for the first game of the season resembled a World XI:

De Goey (Holland),
Petrescu (Romania),
Leboeuf (France),
Desailly (France),
Deschamps (France),
Poyet (Uruguay),
Sutton (England),
Wise (England),
Le Saux (England),
Ferrer (Spain),
Zola (Italy).

Subs used:
Flo (Norway),
Di Matteo (Italy),
Babayaro (Nigeria).

The French trio were all members of the 1998 World Cup-winning side.

In contrast all but three of the Sunderland team were English. Tommy Sorenson (Denmark), Alex Rae (Scotland) and Niall Quinn (Republic of Ireland) being the 'foreigners'.

Despite being beaten four times with goals from Poyet (2), Zola and Flo, Tommy Sorenson was still Sunderland's man of the match.

The Lads are in Town – A Sunderland supporter can't resist a photo opportunity as he comes rushing out of the Brazil cafe before the Chelsea game.

Sunderland supporters at Stamford Bridge for the start of the Premiership campaign.

View From The Bridge

'Now I know how Davy Crockett felt – it was like the Alamo …

I have to say that even at our very best we would have struggled against that Chelsea side.'

Peter Reid

A Blue Day

When Sunderland were drawn against Chelsea for the opening game of the Premiership season it really whetted the appetite. We were now back where we belonged along with the best in the country. No more away trips to Stockport, Crewe or Grimsby – we now had Old Trafford, Anfield and Highbury to look forward to. And kicking off the season at Stamford Bridge, against some of the most famous players in the land, was what fans had been waiting for.

However, in the glorious sunshine of London our dreams were to be shattered. It had been great before the game mixing with the lads from Chelsea. Their fans did have a bad reputation in the past but the ones we spoke to were very friendly even offering to buy us drinks. We joked that it would be a close game but they were convinced that they would hammer us. Most of them, however, did think we would be successful this season – once we had recovered from defeat that day.

How right they were. We were never in the game as the true class of some of their players really showed. Deschamps strolled around as if it was a training session while Zola was tearing through our defence at will. Luckily, Sutton had a string of embarrassing misses that kept the score down to single figures.

The Black Cat at Stamford Bridge before the big kick-off.

Sunderland supporters Neil and Karen Henderson (right) meet up with Chelsea fans Tony Sharp and Sue Hawkins.

The day was complete – for Chelsea fans anyway – when Zola set up Poyet to score one of the goals of the season.

After the game we went to Earls' Court for a drink. Again, there were lots of their fans around who we started talking to. They were all impressed by our supporters. One said he was amazed when Poyet's volley went in to see almost all the Sunderland fans applauding the goal. Another asked why we had black cats on our shirts. Then, when we were all watching TV for the other results, we cheered when Newcastle's defeat was announced and that Alan Shearer had been sent off. One Chelsea fan turned to me to say, 'Well, it hasn't been all bad news today.'

Matthew Johnson

England 2 Belgium 1
10th October 1999 at Stadium of Light, Attendance 40,897

Sunderland had the honour of staging a full England international for the first time in almost fifty years when Belgium visited the Stadium of Light. England captain Alan Shearer was given a great reception by the crowd – surpassed only by that reserved for Kevin Phillips. The national anthems and minute's silence for the Paddington rail crash victims were observed with impeccable respect.

Young 'uns – Even Newcastle shirts were seen.

As the match got underway England made the early going. A Shearer overhead kick game the home side the lead after only six minutes. Kevin Phillips looked sharp and was playing some nice touches. One brilliant back heel set up left winger Steve Guppy but the Leicester man failed to take advantage and the Belgian 'keeper got to the ball first.

Belgium got back into the game with a well worked goal. Sheffield Wednesday's centre forward De Bilde played a fine ball through the England defence and when the ball was pulled back across goal Branko Strupar easily beat Seaman for the equaliser. The half ended with no further addition to the score.

During the interval Sunderland's Swedish international Stefan Schwarz was given a great reception by supporters. The previous day he had helped Sweden

Showing the Flag – These fans leave no doubt to where their allegiances lie.

Showing the Flag – Supporters in the in the North Stand play their part in the pre-match build up.

beat Poland 2-0 thus ensuring England a Euro 2000 play-off place.

After Kevin Keegan's half time dressing-room talk England stepped up the tempo. Midway through the half they re-gained the lead through a superb goal from Jamie Redknapp. The Liverpool midfielder beat the Belgian 'keeper with a left foot pile-driver from 25 yards out. England maintained their lead until the final whistle to record a winning start in their first game at the Stadium of Light.

Local support – A large proportion of Sunderland fans turned out to cheer England.

A weekend that began with fears of impending darkness ended in the Stadium of Light yesterday when England overcame a decent Belgian side with strikes of lightning from Alan Shearer and Jamie Redknapp.

Daily Telegraph, 11th October 1999.

Alan Shearer's zest for the game continues to gather momentum, the England captain scoring his eleventh goal in five games with an athletic overhead kick. Never again will the Geordie be cheered in Sunderland.

The Times, 11th October 1999.

When the fixtures are moved from Wembley, I will be pushing for England to come here again … I thought the reception the two Newcastle players got was a great credit to the Sunderland people.

Kevin Keegan, England coach.

Remember The Roar

Sometime odd games stick in your mind for very little reason. I remember a match at Roker against Watford in the early 1980s. It was the season we first bought Paul Bracewell and he was forming a good partnership with Mark Proctor. I think it was against Watford that we saw the best of those two quality players. We played Watford off the park that day. We won 3-0 and Proctor scored one of the goals. Although my memory of the actual game is a bit sketchy I can still recall the atmosphere in the ground. It wasn't a big attendance but the crowd really made some noise that day – especially in the Roker End which had been relatively quiet during a few seasons of poor football. During one attack the Roker Roar was urging the players forward and you could see them responding to it.

The following Saturday we played West Ham at home. Again The Lads were brilliant. At one point I think the whole of the Roker End was jumping up and down, signing and making more noise than the Fulwell End – almost unheard of! West Ham were hardly in the game until the final minutes when they scored the only goal to clinch a victory they did not deserve. Minutes later, when the final whistle blew, the whole of Roker Park cheered Sunderland from the field. They had not deserved to lose and the crowd showed their appreciation. Where but Sunderland do you get support like that?

Billy Swan

In the last years of Roker Park the Roker End was a shadow of its former self. Reduction in capacity due to demolition and new safety regulations changed the Roker End drastically but even to the end the atmosphere there was special.

HEROES FOREVER

Sunderland players training at Roker Park in the 1950s. This was a time described as the 'Golden Age of Football' but Sunderland supporters have heroes that span all eras.

Terror of the Scots

Alan Morton, the great Rangers and Scotland international, recalled how England had a magnificent side in the early 1920s: 'In her ranks was the terror of Scottish defences – the broad-shouldered, deadly scoring Charlie Buchan. He became a feared man to all Scots because of his superb timing, tempestuous shot on the run, or subtle flick, as effective as the most viciously delivered drive.'

At this time Buchan's goalscoring exploits at Sunderland established him as one of the club's all-time greats.

Quick 'Un

Sunderland's 1937 FA Cup Final full back Jimmy Gorman had electrifying pace. When he was with his previous club Blackburn Rovers he was timed at 5.2 seconds over 50 yards. A time comparable with professional sprinters of the day.

Selling Himself

In January 1949 when Ivor Broadis joined Sunderland he became the first manager to transfer himself. As Carlisle United's player/manager he could not refuse Sunderland's £18,000 offer for his services. He left Brunton Park managerless but with a healthy bank balance. As his successor Carlisle gave the first chance in management to none other than Bill Shankly.

Barney Bircham

Barney Bircham used to play in goal for Sunderland during the last war. At the time my sister Irene was going out with Barney. I used to take her to the matches then afterwards the three of us along with Barney's father would get the tram home to Grangetown.

George Faller

Busy Start

When Bobby Gurney made his first League appearance for Sunderland on Saturday 3rd April 1926 he was to have a busy week ahead of him. After making a scoring debut in a 3-2 defeat at West Ham he played in a 2-0 win at Leeds on the following Tuesday. The next day he turned out against Bolton Wanderers at Brunton Park, Sunderland going down by the odd goal in five. On Saturday 10th April, Arsenal provided the opposition for Bobby Gurney's first game at Roker Park. He scored both goals in a 2-1 victory over the Gunners to end a momentous week for the young Silksworth lad.

Tragic Death

The greatest tragedy in my football career overtook our club when Jimmy Thorpe died. Thorpe was a gentleman on and off the field, and to me his passing was unbelievable.

I well remember the occasion when I went over to Jarrow to sign Thorpe. I met the secretary of the club, and learned that a certain other big club was interested in Thorpe, but as soon as I met the player he himself said, 'If I am going to play for a First League club, it will be in the County of Durham.' Meaning of course, Sunderland.

Johnny Cochrane
Sunderland manager, 1936

Jimmy Thorpe was injured in a goalmouth scramble in the League match against Chelsea at Roker Park on 1st February 1936. Sunderland's young goalkeeper died in hospital four days later.

When We Were Kings

Right: The First Division championship trophy – won in 1995-96 and 1998-99 seasons. When the club claimed the trophy in 1935-36 Sunderland were English champions. This was the sixth occasion Sunderland had claimed football's top prize.

First Division Championships

1891-92
1892-93
1894-95
1901-02
1912-13
1935-36
1995-96 (old Div 2)
1998-99 (old Div 2)

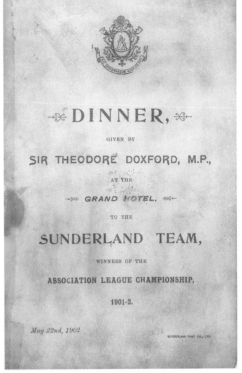

DINNER,

GIVEN BY

SIR THEODORE DOXFORD, M.P.,

AT THE

GRAND HOTEL,

TO THE

SUNDERLAND TEAM,

WINNERS OF THE

ASSOCIATION LEAGUE CHAMPIONSHIP,

1901-2.

May 22nd, 1902

The menu from the dinner to honour Sunderland's championship-winning season of 1901-02.

Hold On Tight

I went to the Stadium of Light to see Sunderland parade the First Division trophy. We were outside the gates when Bob Murray asked me if I wanted to hold the trophy. My mam asked him if he would take a picture. He did and said don't drop it. It's something I will never forget.

Natalie Barraclough

Before the 1936 championship dinner at the New Rink in Sunderland the players were interviewed by Capt. Jack of the *Sunday Sun*. Some of the memorable moments of that triumphant campaign are recalled below.

When I am asked to write about Sunderland's best game last season I have no difficulty in recalling it. It was at Brentford in a miserable, heartbreaking downpour of rain. About 25,000 people turned up to see the League leaders and I couldn't help being sorry for those who were not under cover.

But without boasting, I bet many of them forgot after the first five minutes that they were drenched to the skin.

I was the proudest man in the world to be captain of such a team. Everything was so effortless. The ball went from man to man with amazing precision. Everybody seemed to know just where to find a colleague. The ball was made to do all the work.

We won by five goals to one, and despite the fact that we had given their team a terrible drubbing, the crowd rose as one man and cheered us to the echo.

Alec Hastings

I have no doubt that my colleagues have been talking about games in which they have played, and which have provided many thrills during the past season. I took part in a good number of them, but by way of a change I will refer to a match at which I was a spectator.

I refer to our sensational 5-4 victory against the Arsenal at Roker Park. I saw an amazing exhibition of pure football on that occasion. In the first half one got the impression that the Arsenal was much over-rated, but after the interval we got a taste of what the Arsenal can really do when Dame Fortune, plus their ability, came into the picture.

Sunderland had delighted their supporters with a display of great

The front of the souvenir menu produced for the dinner honouring the 1936 champions.

football which I am sure could hardly have been bettered by what has been described on many occasions as the team of all the talents, and yet, as I say, the Arsenal brought the crowd to its feet by an astonishing fight for supremacy in which they just failed.

There were many goals in this match – indicating a weakness in defence, but to tell the truth a stonewall could not have stopped the goals that were scored on this occasion. On both sides we saw a marvellous display of defensive football.

Bill Murray

The ball came fast and low to me just outside the penalty area, and I went for it at top speed. I managed to hit it in my stride, and it went crashing into the net. I don't think I have ever hit a ball harder. Where was that? At Everton last November. That goal was my biggest thrill of the season. The pass was not meant for me, but for Bob Gurney, but he travelled too fast for it.

We beat Everton that day, the first

victory at Goodison Park for a long spell – another cause for intense satisfaction.

Another game I shall never forget was our 7-2 win at Birmingham on Easter Monday. That game definitely made us League Champions, and the whole team played like champions, as they did also against Arsenal at Roker Park just after Christmas. What a game that was! Sunderland at their best in the first half, and Arsenal superb after the interval. One of my two goals that day was from the penalty spot, which reminds me that during the season I missed a couple of penalties.

Altogether a most memorable season for Sunderland.

Raich Carter

Raich Carter.

Looking back over the season that has now closed, I think that I got my biggest thrills in our match at Brentford, which we won 5-1. Our left wing triangle, Alec Hastings, Jimmy Connor and myself had what is known as a real day out. Everything we tried came off, short passes, long passes, over-head kicks, throw ins, corner-kicks, headers, flicks … I never experienced anything like it.

Our opponents were running all ways but the right way. The second half was all ours, and I thought it was very sporting on the part of the Brentford players, who, as we were leaving the field, clustered around us and complimented our team upon their display. There was no doubt that they had taken their drubbing – without complaint. And their compliments were followed by others from the Brentford officials.

Paddy Gallacher

It was my good fortune to score five goals against Bolton Wanderers at Roker Park, and it was only natural, I think, that I should have felt a bit bucked about this feat.

There were many people who thought that I was not the actual scorer of the fourth … The shot I put

in was 'registering', but Alec Hastings came along to make double sure, but, as he agreed afterwards the ball was just over the line when he banged it to the back of the net.

That day I felt I was the master of that very good Washington friend of mine Atkinson, the Bolton Wanderers centre-half, and yet during the Easter campaign when I met him again – this time at Burnden Park – I could not get a decent kick at the ball.

But some recompense came on Easter Monday when we won that remarkable game at Birmingham to establish our Championship claims. The score was 7-2 for us, and four came from your humble!

Bobby Gurney

I really couldn't tell you which was my biggest thrill during the past season. I know I had a lot – my last minute winner against Huddersfield Town in our last home match, for instance.

Jimmy Connor

I think the game which thrilled me most is that with Blackburn Rovers at Ewood Park, when the score resulted 1-1. On that display by the Rovers, it is really difficult to imagine that the Rovers have to go into the Second Division. They put up a wonderful fight.

First of all Beattie scored, and then Gurney equalised following which it was a ding-dong duel, and near the finish it almost seemed that the Rovers would snatch victory.

Matt Middleton

I felt very proud when I was given my first big chance in the Sunderland team. It was at Portsmouth where the score was 2-2, but this occasion did not provide me with the thrills I got the next Saturday when I was again included in the first team.

In the first place I felt that the Roker Park crowd were ready to give me special encouragement. And they did.

Our opponents were Preston North End. At the interval they were leading 2-1. A few minutes afterwards I put on two. The first I headed through from a long cross by Jimmy Connor, and for the second I had to thank Bobby Gurney. He came towards the inside right position, and then slipped a forward pass which I took in my stride. Then I shot and beat Holdcroft, whom I regard as one of the best goalkeepers I have played against.

I can't really express how delighted I was when I put on those goals, and how proud I was when my colleagues rushed over to shake hands!

Len Duns

I do not think I will ever forget our game at Maine Road when we defeated Manchester City by 1-0. On that occasion I started off at inside-left, but misfortune overtook us. We lost the services of Jimmy Clark through injury, and I dropped back to left-half, Alec Hastings, going into the middle.

What a tussle it was with 10 men against eleven fighting fit. It was an occasion when I had reason to appreciate the sterling qualities of

Eric Brooke who was, as they say, here there and everywhere. Sometimes he was actually throwing in on my side, and how I had to watch his throws!

Eric gave me a tremendous amount of running about. I have never seen a player fight more eagerly for his side, and I will admit quite frankly that I was greatly relieved when 'Raich' Carter deceived the opposition and bringing out Swift from his goal succeeded in scoring the goal that gave us two points.

The tension lasted to the end of the game, Manchester City battling for an equaliser, but our defence holding out. Phew! It was SOME game.

Sandy McNab

As an old campaigner thrills in football are few and far between, yet I shall never forget a certain day early in November last when I became a Sunderland player.

Three or four days later I qualified for a winning bonus, beating Preston at Roker Park. I actually played in 11 games off the reel, and as we won nine of them – you can bet it was one succession of thrills for me.

As for the game which stands out most vividly in my recollections I am not quite sure whether it was our 5-1 win at Brentford or our championship-sealing win at Birmingham by 7-2 on Easter Monday. Both were 'classic' demonstrations of penetrative football, and in both cases I was little more than a spectator.

Tom Morrison

Those Were The Days

The last time Sunderland were champions of England the top division looked very different from that of today. More than half the clubs in 1935-36 are now in lower divisions.

While Sunderland were winning the First Division in 1935-36, mighty Manchester United were winning the Second Division title.

Johnny Mapson

1917-1999

Johnny Mapson, goalkeeper in the 1937 FA Cup Final.

The Reading-born 'keeper in action at Highbury in 1949.

Johnny Mapson punching clear in a match against Blackpool at Roker Park. The great goalie played for Sunderland in three different decades – 1930s, '40s and '50s – all in the First Division.

Sunderland and Scotland 'keeper Willie Fraser beats West Brom's Bobby Robson (present Newcastle manager) to the ball.

Penalty King

The best penalty taker I've seen at Sunderland was Harry Hooper. His kicks used to travel low then rise up into the roof of the net. The 'keeper never knew where the ball was going. When Jimmy Montgomery started at Roker Park he said his ambition was to save a Harry Hooper penalty.

Tommy Turnbull

A Man's Game

Billy Elliott was a hard man in the Sunderland team of the 1950s. In one game he scythed down a player and even the Roker Park crowd gasped. That night I was having a pint in the Roker Hotel when Billy Elliott came up and stood next to me at the bar. I said, 'That tackle was a bit rough today.' He then lifted his shirt and there were stud marks all down his chest. Billy said, 'That's what he gave me in the first half.'

George Faller

Mr Versatile

The most versatile footballer Sunderland have ever had was Willie Watson. He played in almost every position on the field. He played for England at both football and cricket.

Fred Hagel

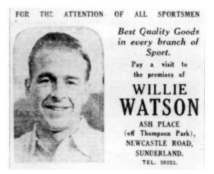

An advert for Willie Watson's sports shop. For years the Sunderland and England man had a shop in the town.

Crowd Pleaser

Shack was a great entertainer. Once he got the ball you knew something was going to happen. Shack's name on the team sheet used to put 10,000 on the gate.

Jackie O'Halloran

The one and only Len Shackleton.

Wearside Legend

I was at Blackpool the day Charlie Hurley made his debut in 1957. I was 14 years old at the time and we were living down High Street East. I remember Freddie Dobson from Wear Garth called round and said there was a place on the coach. My mother gave me the £1 it cost for the trip.

Charlie Hurley had a nightmare start to his Sunderland career when we were hammered 7-0 at Bloomfield Road. Despite a 6-0 drubbing in the next game at Burnley, Charlie went on to establish himself as a legend on Wearside. He was certainly my favourite Sunderland player.

Giant of the Game – Charlie Hurley in a heading duel.

Ray Charlton

Nicky Goes Nap

When Nicky Sharkey scored five goals in the 7-1 win over Norwich in 1963 he was every kid's hero. People still talk about his five goals as if he never played another game for Sunderland. In fact he scored 51 goals in 99 League games for Sunderland – a great strike rate.

Matty Morrison

Dream Player

Colin Todd was the best player I ever saw play for Sunderland. I remember the surging runs he used to make turning defence into attack within seconds. It was a tragedy he left Sunderland when he did. He should have achieved all his dreams at Roker Park.

A youthful Colin Todd.

Richie Ankers

Sunderland and Scotland winger George Mulhall.

Great Winger

In the early 1960s outside left George Mulhall was one of Sunderland's best players. Mulhall could beat a man on a sixpence – he would send the defender the wrong way and he was away down the wing.

Peter Collins

Continental Experience

Irishman Johnny Crossan was Sunderland's equivalent to Denis Law. He could read the game off the ball as well as being a master on it. When I was in the Army in Germany in the early 1960s we used to travel all over Europe to watch games. I remember going to watch Standard Liege with George Mulhall's relation Eric. Johnny Crossan was playing for Standard Liege at the time but little did we realise he would be shortly be playing for Sunderland. Nor did we know George Mulhall would sign for Sunderland a month before Crossan.

Matty Morrison

Topper Tueart

My favourite Sunderland player was Dennis Tueart. The first Sunderland game I went to was against Wolves in 1969 and Tueart scored with a cracking header. The *Football Echo* that night had a picture of Tueart on the front and I remember thinking 'I was there'. Tueart was a topper player.

Keith Hulsmeier

A Gentleman

I thought George Herd was an outstanding player. He had all the skill in the world. Despite his size he was a really strong player. A few years ago I met him and he was a real gentleman.

Richie Ankers

George Herd.

Charlie Hurley makes a presentation before a match at Roker Park in August 1965. The other players (from the front) are: Mike Hellawell, Jimmy McNab, Sandy McLaughlan, John O'Hare and Jim Baxter.

Sunderland players at pre-season training at Cleadon in 1964. How many Roker favourites can you name?

Ahead Of Play

Jim Baxter was a class player. He used to put the ball where the man should have been.

Tommy Turnbull

Buttonhole Baxter

In the early days of the Supporters' shop we often had to improvise to move stock. When we were left with lots of team photographs we could not sell we cut out the heads of players and stuck them on badges. These badges of Jim Baxter, Jimmy Montgomery & Co went like hot cakes.

George Forster

Finesse

The best Sunderland player I've seen was Jim Baxter. The former Rangers man had finesse. He used to stroke passes all over Roker Park.

Peter Collins

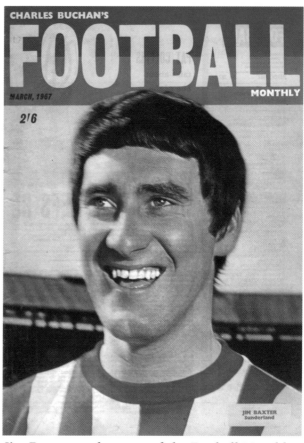

CHARLES BUCHAN'S
FOOTBALL
MONTHLY
MARCH, 1967
2/6

JIM BAXTER
Sunderland

Jim Baxter on the cover of the Football Monthly in 1967.

Great Potential

I thought Harry Hood was a brilliant player. I've never seen anyone with reflexes like the young Scot. I saw him score some spectacular goals. The best was against Manchester United at Roker Park in February 1965. He hammered a tremendous shot from outside the penalty box that ended up in the roof of the net. When Ian McColl took over as manager, Hood's days at Roker were numbered. His potential was clear to see but he was allowed to leave and was later to star for Celtic and Scotland.

Michael Bute

Banana Man

When Bobby Kerr first got into the Sunderland side in the 1960s he was brilliant. I remember he was the first player I saw to hit 'banana' shots around defensive walls.

Michael Stephenson

Classic Centre Forward

The best forward I've seen at Sunderland was Neil Martin. He was great in the air and scored some cracking goals. He was only at Roker for two or three season in the '60s but he left a lasting impression.

Ray Redman

Billy Hughes was a great favourite with Sunderland supporters. *Above* and
below: Two examples of his heading ability at Roker Park in the mid '70s.

Vic Halom tries an acrobatic effort against Manchester United 'keeper Alex Stepney.

Tony Towers converting a penalty kick against Carlisle at Brunton Park in 1976. After his transfer from Manchester City, Towers outstanding performances in the red and white shirt earned him an England call up. He won three caps before moving on to Birmingham City.

A young looking Barry Siddall keeping goal for Bolton at Roker Park. After moving to Sunderland in 1976 Siddall became one of the great characters in the Roker dressing-room.

Rocket Shot

One of the best goals I ever saw at Roker Park was scored by John Hawley. The match was against Arsenal in December 1980. He was about 40 yards out when he hit a shot that beat Pat Jennings. It did not drop over the 'keeper's head but went like a bullet beating him for pace. I think Arsenal later signed Hawley on the strength of that one goal.

Michael Stephenson

Left: John Hawley in action against Newcastle in a friendly. The big striker scored one of the best goals ever seen at Roker Park.

Stars of the '70s

Sunderland had some great players in the 1970s. Shaun Elliott was a tremendous footballer. I never thought he got the recognition at international level he deserved. Kevin Arnott was another player who should have reached the very top. I thought he could have been a better player than Chris Waddle. One player who did win England caps at Sunderland was Tony Towers. But he left Roker for Birmingham when he was at his peak.

Jimmy Smiles

Wembley Jinx

My favourite Sunderland player was Shaun Elliott. The highlight of his career should have been the Milk Cup Final at Wembley in 1985 but he missed the game through suspension. He was certainly a big miss against Norwich.

Phil Reynolds

Arnott & Co

Kevin Arnott was my favourite player. Like all class players he appeared to have plenty of time on the ball. There were a number of outstanding players alongside Arnott in the Sunderland team of the late 1970s and early '80s. Gary Rowell and Shaun Elliott were two of the finest players of all-time.

Bernie Lane

Shaun Elliott.

Cruncher

My favourite Sunderland player was Billy Whitehurst. My choice might surprise some people but I thought he was great. He was hard as nails, a real cruncher in challenges.

Dave Chevington

A Sweet Bit of Play

I always thought Peter Davenport was a very skilful player and was brilliant during our FA Cup run in 1992. His last few years at Sunderland weren't as memorable but he was playing in a poor side. I remember one time when I went to a Youth game at Roker and was sitting in one of the executive boxes. Next to our box were a few of the Sunderland players including Davenport. At half time Davenport was talking to a group of young fans who were below us in the paddock. They had some sweets and Davenport had his hand out of the small window the boxes had and was shouting down for the kids to throw him a sweet. One of them did and amazingly he caught it straight away. All the kids were cheering and Davenport was really pleased with himself. It just goes to show the good hand-eye co-ordination footballers have. I bet the sweets were Midget Gems as well.

Ronnie McGuire

Worthington Special

Although Frank Worthington played less than twenty games in the red and white shirt he was the best Sunderland player I've ever seen. He was sheer class. His first touch was brilliant and the crowd loved him.

He was also a nice guy off the field. We were outside Anfield for a match in 1983 when a police horse trod on the foot of one of my mates. There was uproar with the lad trod on eventually getting arrested for his protests. Frank Worthington saw the incident as he was driving to the players' entrance. He pulled up and told us he would appear as a witness for him if the case went to court. Charges were not pressed and Frank was saved an appearance in court.

Scot Stewart

From Roker To Fino's

Frank Worthington was my favourite Sunderland footballer. He made the ball talk. I used to see him in Fino's night club, he always had a crowd of admirers around him.

Richie Cooney

Benno

I have been watching Sunderland since the late 1970s and in that time my favourite player is Gary Bennett. There can hardly be a player who suffered more highs and lows at Roker than Benno. He played in two Cup Final defeats – and a Play-off – and was in three relegation sides and two promotion sides. He always gave 100 percent. I remember one tackle he made at Roker Park which was the best I ever saw. I can't recall who we were playing against but one of the opposing players was running towards goal when he was stopped in his tracks. Bennett seemed to leap from yards away, get the ball and passed it to one of our players. It was crunching but fair. When he made the challenge the whole of the crowd seemed to rise with a might roar.

Marcus Johnson

Gary Bennett in great demand by youngsters outside Roker Park. The popular defender is now part of the large former Sunderland contingent at Feethams.

Turning Defence into Attack

Sunderland fans seem to have a tradition of taking full backs to their heart. In my time I remember cheering the skills, and sometimes crunching tackles, of Joe Bolton, John Kay, Reuben Agboola and today Chris Makin. From my youth, one full back sticks in my memory for some unknown reason. That player is Joe Hinnigan who I don't think played very many games and certainly wasn't the best defender I ever saw at Roker Park. I remember him for his exploits during one season in the early 1980s. It wasn't a particularly memorable time except for a few games when Hinnigan became our star player. He was not known for his goalscoring talents but in three consecutive games he scored four times – unheard of for a full back especially a Sunderland one. He scored twice in one game at home and seemed to run half the length of the pitch during his celebrations. His goalscoring run soon came to an end when he was sent off in his following game. After these heady heights his career at Roker went down hill and he was eventually transferred to a lower league club. I can still picture the celebrations both on and off the pitch when he scored. I expect similar scenes when Chris Makin eventually finds the net.

Billy Swan

Joe 90

The best left back I've seen at Sunderland in the last thirty years has been Joe Bolton. We used to stand in the Paddock and the crowd used to roar 'Go on Joe' and he would go into crunching tackles. I'm sure 90% of wingers jumped out of challenges.

Michael Stephenson

Joe Bolton – a great all-round defender.

Roker favourite John Kay shoots for goal against Middlesbrough at Ayresome Park in 1990.

Chris Makin in action against Huddersfield in October 1997. Some people might think the Stadium of Light crowd are booing the full back when he goes forward with the ball. But the roar is: 'Shoot, Shoot' encouraging him to get on the scoresheet for the first time.

Lionel Perez

I live just north of London, but still try to travel to as many home games as possible. In the 1996-97 season, I held a season ticket and made the eight hour round rail trip from my home to Sunderland time and time again. On the return leg of one excursion, I couldn't help but notice that the bloke sitting a few seats away looked a bit like Lionel Perez, Sunderland's then eccentric French goalkeeper. I wasn't absolutely sure that it was him, because his long hair was swept back, and he was wearing casual clothes – like most fans, I'd only ever seen footballers in their strips, or post-match suits! Anyway, I was sitting next to another Sunderland fan that I had met several times on my travels, and so we embarked on a game of 'is it, isn't it?' Just as I became sure that it was indeed our goalkeeper, my friend would declare that it definitely wasn't. Then, he wouldn't be so sure himself, but I'd go and change my mind regardless. This went on for half an hour or so. It seems ridiculous, thinking back, but the bloke really looked different off the pitch. We finally became sure that it was Lionel when he pulled a French newspaper out of his bag and began reading.

Lionel Perez in the Roker Park dressing-room with pupils from Hasting Hill School.

That was the end of our debate and the next couple of hours passed without incident. Neither of us approached Perez, because, well, what do you say? And anyway, players must get sick of being hassled by strangers. However, when returning from the buffet bar, I suddenly realised that the great man was walking down the aisle of the carriage before me – coming my way. Considering the fact that I was wearing a Sunderland shirt, and that Lionel had just been unveiled as the fans' player of the month the previous day (getting my vote, as it happens), I felt I must say something as we passed. I reckoned that something along the lines of, 'Well done on your recent displays,' or 'Keep up the good work,' would have been suitable. Anyway, the moment of truth arrived and Lionel stood before me in that little space between carriages. He took one look at my shirt and smiled. Although I'd just rehearsed in my head what I was going to say, his gesture suddenly became the signal for me to make a fool of myself. I inexplicably held out my hand, which he took and shook, but I was unable to say anything for a moment of two. Then, I muttered, 'Monsieur Perez?' to which he replied, 'Yes,' and I continued, 'Hello.' He smiled again, just a little confused by my rather strange line in communication, and we parted.

When I got back to my seat, my friend, realising that Lionel and I must have passed, excitedly asked what I'd said. I told him I'd said, 'Hello.'

'Yeah, and then what,' he asked.

And then nothing I replied. Nothing? How could I have stopped to speak to one of our star players and said nothing? I guess, like many a star-struck youngster before me, I just froze at the eleventh hour. I was twenty-eight years old at the time.

Neil Henderson

Alex Rae in the thick of the action.

Sunderland players relaxing after a game.

Nicky Summerbee has brought back old fashioned wing play to Sunderland.

Princes of Denmark

Kim Heiselberg was Sunderland's first Danish signing. The young midfielder's £125,000 transfer from Esbjerg did not work out and he returned to Denmark.

Above: Since his transfer from OB Odense, Tommy Sorenson has become one the most popular players with Sunderland supporters.

Left: Carsten Fredgaard is taking longer to establish himself after his move from Denmark.

Great Dane

Sunderland's Danish players are by no means the first to appear in England's top flight. Either side of the First World War Nils Middleboe turned out as an amateur for Chelsea.

The Danish international played in the 1-1 draw against Sunderland at Stamford Bridge on 13th December 1913. The *Echo* reported: 'Middleboe appeared to have the measure of Buchan and Mordue, and if he did not always prevent them from getting away he was generally about when it came to defence, his towering figure being in the thick of the fray.'

The retention of his amateur status allowed Middleboe to lead his country in the Olympic Games. Denmark under Middleboe's captaincy were twice denied the gold medal by Great Britain. On the second occasion in Stockholm in 1912 former Sunderland goalkeeper Ron Brebner was in the side that beat the Danes.

Years after retiring from the game Middleboe selected a team of the best players he had encountered during his career in England. Sunderland's Charlie Buchan was his selection for the inside right position in his 'Dream Team'.

Shoot-Out of the Marksmen

The goalscoring exploits of Kevin Phillips over the last couple of seasons have sent people rushing to the record books. The name of the man who Super Kev's goals have surpassed is none other than Brian Clough.

Brian Clough was already an established goalscorer when he arrived at Sunderland from Middlesbrough for a £45,000 fee in July 1961. Kevin Phillips was a virtual unknown when Watford were paid £650,000 for his services in the summer of 1997.

The first two seasons each striker spent at Sunderland have some remarkable similarities.

Both players had spells in minor league football before finding success. Clough played for Great Broughton, South Bank and Billingham Sinthonia before going to Ayresome Park. After being released by Southampton as YTS trainee Phillips turned out for Baldock Town before being transferred to Watford for a £10,000 fee.

The goal-hungry pair wasted no time in making their mark on Wearside. Cloughie scored on his League debut for Sunderland in a 4-3 defeat at Walsall. While Phillips was also on the mark in his League debut against Manchester City in a 3-1 victory.

The goals continued to flow as Clough found the net 34 times in League and Cup games and Phillips 35 times (including Play-off games).

Their exploits were still not sufficient to help Sunderland to

Brian Clough	Kevin Phillips
Height 5ft 10$^{1}/_{2}$ in	Height 5ft 7in
Weight 11st 1lb	Weight 11st

Kevin Phillips, Sunderland and England.

promotion to the top flight. In 1961-62 despite a Clough goal in a 1-1 draw in the last game at Swansea, Sunderland missed out by one point.

In 1998-99 a Phillips goal in the Play-off Final at Wembley just failed to ensure promotion.

The goal poachers second season at Sunderland were both ravaged by injury. Both men got off the mark in opening day victories. Two goals for Clough against his former Middlesbrough teammates and a Phillips' penalty against Queens Park Rangers got Sunderland off to home wins. In the early months of the campaign Clough's scoring record was even better than in his first season. Going into the Boxing Day match against Bury he had notched

Brian Clough	Kevin Phillips
1st Season at Sunderland 1961-62	*1st Season at Sunderland 1997-98*
Goals	Goals
29 in 34 League games	29 in 43 League games
5 in 9 Cup games	4 in 2 Cup games
	2 in 3 Play-offs

The Football Echo view of Brian Clough's remarkable goalscoring at the end of March 1962. He went on to score 6 more times in the last 7 games.

24 goals in 23 League games plus a goal a game in 4 League Cup ties. A challenge with Bury 'keeper Chris Harker effectively ended the Sunderland centre forward's career. After scoring 8 goals in 10 League and Cup games Phillips injured a toe in the League Cup tie against Chester City. The injury kept him out of action for four months. He marked his return with a goal at Queen's Park Rangers. He still finished the season with 25 League and Cup goals.

In the 1962-63 season a draw in the last game against Chelsea at Roker would have given Sunderland promotion. But defeat at the hands of Tommy Docherty's Pensioners

snatched this away. Clough's injury midway through the campaign was certainly the biggest factor in denying the club promotion. In contrast Phillips' goals helped Sunderland to gain admission to the top flight by a record points total in 1998-99.

Brian Clough won two full England caps. He made his debut in the 1-1 draw against Wales on 17th October 1959, aged 24 years 7 months.

Kevin Phillips at the time of going to print has two England caps. He made his first appearance in the 1-1 draw against Hungary, aged 25 years 9 months.

Both strikers played their first England game alongside teammates who were also making their international debut. Clough's Boro teammate Edwin Holliday and Mickey Gray were the men also honoured for the first time.

Clough gained only one further cap – in the 3-2 defeat against Sweden 11 days after his debut.

Sunderland's Stadium of Light was the setting for Kevin's second cap against Belgium. Hopefully, unlike Cloughie, he has a long international career ahead of him.

Brian Clough promoting his autobiography on the Roker Park pitch he once graced.

Brian Clough 2nd Season at Sunderland 1962-63	Kevin Phillips 2nd Season at Sunderland 1998-99
Goals	Goals
24 in 24 League games	23 in 26 League games
4 in 4 Cup games	0 in 1 Cup games

Unlike Kevin Phillips, there was no way back for Brian Clough from his injury. Although he did return to play in 3 First Division games (1 goal) his playing career was over and a new one in management was about to begin.

Goalscorer Supreme

Without doubt the best goalscorer I've seen was Brian Clough. He would score goals from any angle and from any distance.

I was at the game against Bury when he received the injury that was to finish his career. I thought at first it was just an innocuous challenge. He never got up and when the stretcher was called we knew it was more serious. Even when he was carried off we never dreamed this would signal the end of his playing days.

Ray Charlton

Sad Day

I knew straight away that Cloughie was seriously injured in the match against Bury. The pitch in parts was like concrete that day.

Matty Morrison

Ambrose Fogarty looks anxiously over Brian Clough as he is helped on to a stretcher after the collision with the Bury 'keeper.

St John Ambulancemen carry off the Sunderland centre forward on that fateful Boxing Day.

Only Blackness

Brian Clough recalled the injury:

'I sprinted across the heavy, muddy surface towards the ball, my eye on it … suddenly it was as if someone had just turned out the light. The Bury goalkeeper, Chris Harker, had gone down for the ball, and his shoulder crunched into my right knee. I was slightly off-balance, with my head down. If I'd seen him coming I might have been inclined to kick his head off, but I didn't see him. My head hit the ground, and for a second or two I didn't know a thing. Only blackness.'

Clough The Autobiography

A Last Farewell

A crowd of 31,898 went to Brian Clough's testimonial at Roker Park in October 1965. Stars like Ian St John, Tony Hateley and George Eastham turned out for the Sunderland goalscoring great.

Super Kev

When Phillips was injured against Spurs, the crowd's reaction was amazing. When he went down the first time, with what seemed to be a bad knock, everyone seemed to be on their feet, straining to get a view of the condition of our star striker. Visions went through our minds of how serious the injury could be. There was a silence over the stadium – not a word from over 40,000 fans. Then chants of 'Super Kev' started, slowly getting louder and louder. You could feel the relief go around the ground when he slowly got to his feet. 'He's alright,' people mumbled to themselves or to their neighbours – followed by a thunderous round of applause. I thought it was a moment of high drama.

Stephen Morrissey

Stars of the future – Michael Proctor (above) and Chris Lumsdon (below).

PREMIER CLUBS
REVISITED

Arsenal

Strange Games Against The Gunners

Most games against Arsenal seem to have unusual incidents. The first game I ever saw against the Gunners was when John Hawley scored from about 30 yards out. Today there are plenty of players who try long range strikes but in those days it wasn't so common. Sunderland had the ball in the Arsenal half and there seemed to be nothing happening when all of a sudden the ball was in the back of the net. I was standing right behind the goal in the Roker End and the ball went in like a rocket. Pat Jennings, one of the best goalies in the country, didn't have a chance of stopping it. Not long after, Hawley moved to Highbury but never repeated his goalscoring exploits.

Another strange game against Arsenal was when we played them at about 5 o'clock one Saturday afternoon towards the end of the 1990-91 season. The Londoners were going for the title that season while we were battling against relegation. This was at the time when live games were shown on ITV and the match was moved to suit the TV companies. The game itself wasn't particularly interesting, finishing 0-0, but there was a nice touch at the end. Some of the Sunderland fans chanted 'Champions' for the Arsenal supporters while they returned the compliment with cries of 'Staying up'. Alas it was not to be and Sunderland were relegated the following week with emotional scenes at Maine Road.

In recent years we have had Denis Bergkamp score a wonder goal at Roker while Tony Adams gave us a victory with an own goal. However, the most bizarre game I have ever witnessed was at Highbury in 1996. It was the game where Martin Scott and Paul Stewart were sent off and Peter Reid was ordered from the touch line – all this in the first half. So with our nine men we had to

---

OLD BOYS

Bould, Shack, Quinn ...

Steve Bould's performances for Sunderland in the Premiership have silenced those who said the former Arsenal man was too long in the tooth for the top flight. After going to Highbury from his hometown club Stoke in 1988, the rugged centre half went on to become part of Arsenal's legendary defence. A string of immaculate displays in the red and white shirt have laid an early claim as Sunderland's 'Player of the Season'.

Steve Bould

Len Shackleton was a ground staff boy at Highbury for one season just before the last war. Arsenal told him he would not make the grade and let him go. Others who have played for both clubs include: Jackie Mordue, Charlie Buchan, Dave Halliday, Ray Daniel, Joe Baker, Brian Chambers, John Hawley, Lee Chapman, Niall Quinn and Stefan Schwarz.

hold out for the rest of the game.
Sunderland were well organised in the
second half but very rarely had the ball at
the Arsenal end. At one point Mickey
Gray was running down the wing and
when he reached the half way line
realised that no other Sunderland player
was joining him in the attack. So just
inside the Arsenal half he stopped and
booted the ball out for a throw in near
the corner flag. I suppose there was
nothing else he could do. The Sunderland
fans were singing, 'We've only got nine
men … We've only got nine men.' It was
the first time I had heard that chant and it
was a rare humourous moment that lifted
the gloom. Just when it looked like we
were going to hold out, and earn a well-
deserved draw, Arsenal scored a couple of
goals. Michael Bridges was brought on to
give us an attacking option and nearly
scored. I reckon if he had been brought
on earlier we would have sneaked a draw.

Marcus Johnson

A youthful Steve Bould in Stoke
City colours prior to joining
Arsenal.

Niall Quinn going for goal against Sheffield United at the Stadium of Light.

Aston Villa

A Game of One Half

Sunderland's League game at Villa Park on 11th January 1958 had a remarkable first half. There were seven goals – including a hat-trick from a full back. Villa right back Stan Lynn converted a 4th minute penalty. Myerscough increased the home side's lead in the 11th minute before Colin Grainger reduced the deficit two minutes later. Charlie Fleming grabbed an equaliser after 23 minutes. Lynn scored his second goal again from the penalty spot on the half hour to restore Villa's lead. Sewell made it 4-2 after 34 minutes and Lynn completed his hat-trick 8 minutes later. In the second half, despite Sunderland pressing to get back in the match, there was no addition to the score.

Bosnich the Saviour

I couldn't believe the size and condition of Mark Bosnich when he signed for Manchester United. When I see him like that I can't believe he is the same player who single-handedly kept Aston Villa in the game when we played them in the League Cup in 1993. Don Goodman and Phil Gray were playing up front and they had been outstanding in the previous tie in the competition against Leeds. But try as they might against Villa there was no getting past Bosnich. He was outstanding and I can still remember one save from a Gordon Armstrong header. Armstrong was known for his heading ability and his effort seemed destined for the top corner. But somehow Bosnich leapt and tipped the ball away. I was standing in the Fulwell End that night and there was a bloke next to me with a mobile phone and he was obviously giving someone a full commentary of the game. The Fulwell End was making so much noise that night he would have been struggling to be heard. Villa won 4-1 and even their manager at the time, Ron Atkinson, said Sunderland should have won the game.

Ronnie McGuire

OLD BOYS

Kubicki, Ford, O'Neil ...

Polish international full back Dariusz Kubicki first tried his luck in English football with Aston Villa. He arrived at Villa Park in 1991 from Legia Warsaw for £200,000. After losing his place at Villa he was snapped up by Sunderland in 1994. His consistent form gave him a long run in the Sunderland team before losing his place to Gareth Hall. He showed his versatility by playing half a season at left back when Martin Scott was injured. After moving on to Wolves, Dariusz continued his links with Wearside by carrying on his degree started at the University of Sunderland.

Dariusz Kubicki

Sunderland had to pay a record £30,000 transfer fee to secure the services of Aston Villa's Trevor Ford in 1950. The Welsh international centre forward's stay at the Bank of England Club was to last just three years. In that time he scored 67 goals in 108 League appearances. Others who have played for both clubs include: W.M. Watkins, Alan O'Neil and Tommy Mitchinson.

Above: Australian international Mark Bosnich claims the ball in the League (Coca Cola) Cup tie at Roker in 1993. The Villa 'keeper had an outstanding game, pulling off a string of brilliant saves. *Below*: Gordon Armstrong slides in on Ray Houghton in the same match.

Bradford City

Jamie Lawrence

During a brief stay on Wearside, Jamie Lawrence made a handful of appearances in the red and white shirt. Although speedy and skilful he was still a long way from the finished article. When he was allowed to leave he went on to make a name for himself in the game. He moved to Doncaster for a £20,000 fee and was then transferred to Leicester City for £250,000. Chris Kamara then stepped in to take Lawrence to Valley Parade. He helped Bradford to win promotion in 1998-99 and though plagued by injury, the former Sunderland man has played in a number of the Bantams Premiership games.

Jamie Lawrence during his Roker Park days.

OLD BOYS

Beagrie, Waddle, Lawrence ...

Peter Beagrie is a vital member of Bradford's team as they try to keep their Premier League status. Although the little winger was only at Sunderland on loan he made a big impression on supporters. After joining his hometown club Middlesbrough in 1983 he went on play for Sheffield United, Stoke City and Everton. His wing play was recognised at international level when he played for England at Under 21 and 'B' level. In the 1998-99 season he helped Bradford to join Sunderland in promotion to the Premier League.

Peter Beagrie

The breakdown of Martin Scott's transfer to Bradford City in the summer of '99 robbed the injury-plagued full back of the chance to resurrect his career at Valley Parade. Instead the unlucky defender had to undergo his 16th operation in three years and the fight back to full fitness. Others who have played for both clubs include: Mick Gilhooley, Len Shackleton and Chris Waddle.

Cup Upset

When Sunderland were in the old First Division in 1969 they were drawn against Third Division Bradford City in the League Cup. The Second Round tie at Roker Park on 3rd September was to produce a major upset with the Bantams winning 2-1.

Missing from the Sunderland line-up was the brilliant Colin Todd who had been injured at Old Trafford a few days before.

The visitors made the early running and it was no surprise when Bannister gave them the lead. In the second half Bradford went further ahead before Sunderland pulled a goal back. From a Billy Hughes cross Dennis Tueart managed to reduce the arrears. With half an hour to go Sunderland pushed for an equaliser that never came.

Busy Christmas

On Christmas Day 1940 Len Shackleton turned out for Bradford Park Avenue against Leeds United on the morning and then as a guest for Bradford City against Huddersfield on the afternoon.

Double Hero

As the First Division campaign moved into its final stages, Sunderland's visit to Valley Parade in March 1999 was a real top of the table 'six pointer'. Roared on by their travelling army of supporters Sunderland took the lead in the 71st minute through a Niall Quinn header. Within minutes the big Irishman was donning the goalkeeper's jersey. Tommy Sorenson was concussed in a collision with Bradford's Lee Mills and had to leave the field. For the last twenty minutes of the game Sunderland's defence stifled Bradford's attack to such a degree that Niall Quinn was a virtual spectator. When he was called into action he was given tremendous encouragement from the Sunderland supporters in the crowd.

The victory meant Sunderland went 12 points clear of Ipswich and 15 points ahead of Bradford. The Premiership was in sight.

After an overnight stay in hospital, Tommy Sorenson soon recovered to help Sunderland complete promotion in record-breaking style.

Different Class

Sunderland were flying high in the Premier when they visited Valley Parade on 2nd October 1999. The Sunderland contingent in the 18,204 crowd were soon celebrating when Alex Rae's low shot found the corner of the net. In the second half a close range header from Niall Quinn extended the lead. Sunderland were now in complete control and with a couple of minutes remaining Kevin Phillips forced the ball home. Sunderland continued in search of goals. Super Kev was knocked over by Bradford 'keeper Walsh and converted the spot kick himself.

The final whistle blew to the roar of Red and White supporters at Valley Parade and at the Stadium of Light for the beam back.

The gulf in class between Sunderland and Bradford had clearly grown in the seven months since the sides last met. The 4-0 victory pushed Sunderland into second spot in the Premier behind Manchester United. While the Yorkshire club languished third from bottom, just above Newcastle.

Chelsea

Bryan Robson going in where Chelsea boots are flying in a match at Roker Park on 16th August 1975. The game was Ian Porterfield's first outing for eight months after suffering serious injury in a car crash. The Cup Final hero was later to become manager at Stamford Bridge.

The programme for Sunderland's visit to Stamford Bridge on 14th November 1936. The reigning League champions proved too strong for Chelsea. Goals from Gurney, Duns and Burbanks gave Sunderland a comfortable 3-1 victory.

OLD BOYS

Hall, Walker, Buchan ...

Former Chelsea man Gareth Hall had an uphill battle to win over Sunderland supporters when he replaced the popular Dariusz Kubicki in the side. He retained the right back spot until the end of the 1996-97 season. The Welsh international has since moved on to Swindon.

Clive Walker was a great favourite with supporters of both Sunderland and Chelsea. His dribbling skill, distribution and eye for goal made him one of the top players of the 1970s and '80s. On Sky's Soccer AM the morning of Sunderland's first game back in the Premiership, Chelsea fan Tim Lovejoy asked a group of Sunderland supporters, 'Doesn't Clive Walker still play for you?' Others who have played for both clubs include:

Gareth Hall

Charlie Buchan who turned out at Stamford Bridge during the First World War, Ron Brebner, Geoff Butler, Colin Waldron and Bryan Robson.

Above: Chelsea's Ian Hutchinson goes close with a header in the League match against Sunderland at Stamford Bridge on 20th December 1975. Hutchinson was famous for his long throw-ins. *Below*: Vic Halom helps Jeff Clarke to combat one such throw in the same match.

Coventry City

The Giant Killers

I was at a friend's wedding in the midlands when the bride's father started talking about football. He was a Coventry supporter and told us about one game he remembered at Highfield Road against Sunderland in the early 1960s. It was in the FA Cup when Coventry were in the Third Division and Sunderland were in the Second. Jimmy Hill was the manager and was just starting to put the side together which he would eventually see promoted to the First Division – where they've stayed ever since. He told us how he thought the Sunderland side in those days were one of the 'big' teams with players like Charlie Hurley and Jimmy Montgomery. I had never heard of this game and asked what the score was – being the 'big' side we must have hammered them I thought. 'We won, of course,' he said with pride that had not diminished in the past thirty years. Typical!

Billy Swan

Double Knock-Out

After Sunderland had drawn with Coventry in the League Cup in a great match at Roker in 1990 there was to be disappointment in the return at Highfield Road. Sunderland were beaten 5-0 but that wasn't the worst thing about that night. Billy Hardy had a world championship fight at Crowtree and he was defeated on points. So Sunderland had been beaten twice in one night. Even for long suffering Wearsiders this seemed to be too much to bear.

Ronnie McGuire

OLD BOYS

Butcher, Pickering, Wallace ...

England stalwart Terry Butcher was appointed player/manager at Coventry in November 1990. The former Ipswich and Glasgow Rangers defender's stay at Highfield Road was to prove brief and by 1992 he was playing for Sunderland. Singapore-born Butcher replaced Malcolm Crosby as manager at Roker Park but he in turn made way for MIck Buxton.

Before Kevin Phillips was capped against Hungary in 1999, Nick Pickering had been the last Sunderland player to play for England. Coventry paid £250,00 in 1986 for his services. Nick finished his career at Darlington and today covers football for Radio Newcastle.

Kevin Ball was an apprentice at Coventry

Terry Butcher

City but joined Portsmouth before breaking through to the Sky Blues first team. Others who have played for both clubs include: Harry Buckle, Ken Chisholm, Neil Martin, Jim Holton, Ian Wallace and Sam Allardyce.

Eric Gates shares a joke with Coventry 'keeper Steve Ogrizovic in the League Cup tie in January 1990.

Eye-Opener

When I was in my early twenties my eyesight was getting pretty bad but I put off going to the optician until Sunderland played Coventry in the League Cup in 1990. That was a cracking game with the highlight for most of us being Gary Bennett's bust up with David Speedie. The whole of Roker Park was in uproar as Bennett knocked the Coventry striker into the Clock Stand Paddock.

I was really straining to see what was going on and felt I had missed a vital incident. The following day I made an appointment for an eye test and had a pair of gleaming spectacles for the next home match. Never again was I to miss any action. Although, with some of the football I have witnessed over the years I sometimes wish I hadn't bothered with the glasses.

Stephen Morrissey

David Speedie makes the long lonely walk to the dressing-room after being sent off.

Derby County

Derby County's League visit to Roker Park in 1988-89. Left to right: Peter Shilton, Colin Pascoe, Dickie Ord and Mick Harford.

Pride of Place

It was great at Derby when we won 5-0 in September 1999. All the Sunderland fans were chanting, 'Can we play you every week.' Most of the Derby supporters left when the third goal went in. Then one of their fans ran on the pitch and threw his season ticket down.

After the game there were loads of very friendly people who really made an effort and came up to us and said, 'I know you beat us but we would like to shake your hand.'

It was really windy when we left the ground and one of the Derby fans said this will make you feel at home. They must think we're from the moon.

Tracy Ahmed

OLD BOYS

Gabbiadini, Todd, Carter ...

Marco Gabbiadini was a huge favourite with the Roker crowd. After he joined Sunderland from York City he formed a deadly partnership with Eric Gates which helped Sunderland rise from the Third to the First Division. When Crystal Palace's £1.7 million offer for the England B international was accepted it came as a bombshell to supporters. He was only in London for a short period before he was on his way to the Baseball Ground. Marco is back in the North East now scoring goals for Darlington.

John O'Hare and Colin Todd had to leave Roker Park for the Baseball Ground before gaining full international recognition. Others

Marco Gabbiadini

who have played for both clubs include: Raich Carter, Roy Greenwood, Billy Hughes, Leighton James, Rob Hindmarch, Terry Curran, Dave Watson and Mick Harford.

The Return of the Prodigal Father-in-law

My father-in-law, Barry, lives near Derby and when we played them in 1999 I arranged to stay with him for the weekend and go with him to the game. It was the first Sunderland match he had been to since the 1973 Cup Final. He still had his ticket. We met some of his friends who are Derby fans before the game. They started talking about the time we were beaten 5-0 a few years before. This time it would be our turn to go nap. We arranged to meet them in the pub after the game but only one turned up – his wife had gone straight home but he wanted to prove he could take it. When we walked into the pub a group of their fans gave us a round of applause.

That night, Barry couldn't believe the game he had watched. He spent most of the night giggling to himself. His local newsagent was convinced Derby would win. When I went to buy the local sports paper, *The Green*, the newsagent said he was going to cancel the papers that night because he thought none of the locals would buy them. I told him, 'I'll buy everyone you've got.'

Andrew Pace

You're Not Singing Anymore

At the beginning of the Derby game their fans were singing, 'You're in the wrong division … You're in the wrong division.' By the end of the game we returned the compliment. Although there wasn't too many of their supporters left to hear us. The best part of that great win over Derby was on the Monday when I opened the *Sun* and there was a picture of me at Pride Park with other Sunderland fans celebrating Kevin Phillips' third goal.

Tariq Ahmed

Everton

Late Night At Everton

Most of the games I have seen away from Roker Park have either been at Wembley or when Sunderland played in the FA Cup semi-final. One of the first 'proper' away games I went to was at Goodison Park in the Worthington Cup in November 1998. At Everton we were in a stand very much like the Main Stand at Roker Park. The noisiest home fans were behind one of the goals and the two sets of supporters were very near to each other. The banter between the two fans was great and at times the game was irrelevant because the real entertainment was between the supporters.

The facilities at Goodison Park seem very basic compared to the Stadium of Light. I suppose it's like Roker Park used to be. At half time I went to find a toilet and had to walk the length of the stand to find the ladies. I suppose when the stand was built not many women went to football matches.

The game seemed to go on for ever. The match kicked off late, then with extra time and penalties we didn't get away until about 11.15. Then our bus driver went the wrong way down the motorway and so we didn't get home till about 4 o'clock in the morning. A few people were left behind by our coach. The police just ordered people on to the coaches and then told them to drive off. One lad who didn't make it back to our coach had left his sandwiches – they were soon passed around.

Tracy Ahmed

OLD BOYS

Oster, McCann, Bracewell ...

Former Evertonian Peter Reid went back to his old club to sign John Oster for the start of the 1999-2000 season. Everton signed the winger from Grimsby as a teenager. In two years at Goodison he found it difficult to get a decent run in the first team despite a number of match-winning performances. Still only 20 years old, he joined Sunderland in August 1999 in the hope of re-launching his Premier and international career. He will hope to follow in the footsteps of his former Everton team-mate Gavin McCann who has become a first team regular at the Stadium of Light.

John Oster

In his prime there was no better midfielder in England than Paul Bracewell. Along with Peter Reid he formed a formidable Everton midfield engine room. He had three separate spells at Sunderland and skippered the side in the 1992 FA Cup Final. Others who have played for both clubs include: L.R. Roose, Jack Hedley, Billy Bingham, Colin Todd, Rod Belfitt, Mick Buckley, Ian Atkins and Terry Curran.

Everton provided the opposition for the last ever League game at Roker Park.

Goodison Shoot Out

Duncan Ferguson was playing that night in the Worthington Cup and at every Everton corner Niall Quinn came back to mark him – he got nothing out of Niall that night. At that time there was a rumour that Sunderland were going to buy Ferguson but that week we bought Gavin McCann from Everton instead. Ferguson eventually went to Newcastle and I think we got the best deal. Michael Bridges put us into the lead then a John Collins' free kick brought Everton level. Then young Michael Proctor came on as substitute and almost won the game for us. The game finished 1-1 then went into extra time and then penalties. Everton's Bakayoko missed the penalty to send us through into the next round.

Tariq Ahmed

Tariq and Tracy Ahmed on their travels with Sunderland.

Leeds United

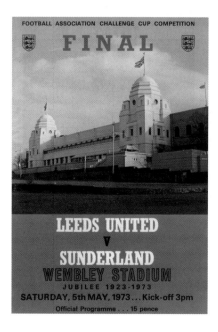

FOOTBALL ASSOCIATION CHALLENGE CUP COMPETITION

FINAL

LEEDS UNITED
v
SUNDERLAND
WEMBLEY STADIUM
JUBILEE 1923-1973
SATURDAY, 5th MAY, 1973...Kick-off 3pm
Official Programme . . . 15 pence

Cup Memories

The highlight of Sunderland v Leeds United encounters has to be the FA Cup triumph in 1973. The 'David v Goliath' clash captured the imagination of the whole country (and beyond). There was little sympathy from neutrals when Goliath was slain by the underdogs.

Sunderland supporters had bitter memories of the FA Cup clash with Leeds six years before. Roker fans thought their name was on the trophy that year with wins over Brentford (5-2) and Peterborough (7-1) in earlier rounds. Leeds held no fears for a side including Jim Baxter, Monty, Colin Todd, John O'Hare and Neil Martin. It took three games, one broken leg (Bobby Kerr), a disputed penalty and two sendings off (George Herd and George Mulhall) before Leeds got through.

OLD BOYS

Bridges, Gray, Revie ...

Michael Bridges' £5 million transfer to Elland Road saddened many Sunderland supporters. It was hoped the hugely talented young striker would finally fulfil his potential in the Premiership with Sunderland. Instead Leeds are reaping the benefit of his Sunderland apprenticeship. After making a sensational breakthrough into the first team when only 17 Michael soon attracted the attention of national team coaches. In the four seasons afterwards he could never establish a regular place in the side. When the England Under 21 international was put on the transfer list a posse of Premiership clubs were on his trail. In the end Michael opted to join David O'Leary's young squad of players at Elland Road.

Michael Bridges

Scottish international Frank Gray made over 300 League appearances for Leeds (in two spells) before joining Sunderland in 1985. Frank's elder brother Eddie played against Sunderland in the 1973 FA Cup Final. Others who have played for both clubs include: Eddie Burbanks, Ken Willingham, Ken Chisholm, Jack Overfield, Colin Grainger, Don Revie, Wayne Entwistle, John Hawley, Lee Chapman, Frank Worthington and Chris Turner.

Above: Action from the League (Coca Cola) Cup tie at Roker Park on 21st September 1993. The first leg match ended in a 2-1 victory with goals from Don Goodman and Phil Gray. *Below*: Leeds full back Tony Dorigo fires in a free kick at goal in the same match.

Leicester City

Going in to the last game of the 1957-58 season Sunderland and Leicester City were in desperate trouble at the foot of the First Division. Former Sunderland goalscoring hero of the '20s Dave Halliday was the Leicester manager at this time.

Sunderland beat Portsmouth in the last match at Fratton Park and if Leicester lost at Birmingham, Sunderland would have stayed up.

Sunderland did their part by beating Portsmouth 2-0 with a brace from South African-born Don Kichenbrand. However, Birmingham City were beaten 1-0 at St Andrews thus condemning Sunderland to the Second Division for the first time since entering the League in 1890.

With two going down Sheffield Wednesday finished bottom on 31 points. Sunderland finished on 32 points, the same as Newcastle United and Portsmouth, but they avoided the drop on goal average.

Having escaped relegation Leicester stayed in the top flight for another 11 seasons. They were relegated in 1968-69 when they were also beaten in the FA Cup Final. A feat similar to Sunderland's League Cup Final/relegation double in 1985.

OLD BOYS

Agnew, Whitworth, Worthington ...

Steve Agnew joined Leicester City from Blackburn Rovers, having started his career with Barnsley. He then left Filbert Street for Roker Park and helped Sunderland to promotion in 1996. The hard tackling midfielder never quite made it as a regular at Sunderland. When it seemed he was going to establish himself in the team he was hit by injury. He later moved on to York City.

Steve Agnew

A trio of former Leicester player turned out for Sunderland in the late 1970s and early '80s. England full back Steve Whitworth and Bob Lee joined Sunderland from Filbert Street for large transfer fees. Another England man, Frank Worthington, found himself at Roker via a roundabout route near the end of his career. Others who have played for both clubs include: Jock Paterson, Bert Davis, Ken Chisholm, Don Revie, Nicky Sharkey, Billy Hughes and Dave Buchanan.

Gary Bennett in action against Leicester City at Roker Park in 1989.

Craig Russell fires in a shot on the Leicester City goal while future Sunderland player Steve Agnew looks on.

Liverpool

Mersey Curse

Liverpool is one of those teams that Sunderland seem never to get any joy from. Whereas against most of the top sides – like Manchester United, Arsenal and Leeds – we have memorable victories to savour, there's not many times we have turned over the 'Mighty Reds'. I think our run of poor form against them started in 1970 when Sunderland had to win their last game at home to Liverpool to ensure they stayed in the old First Division. A late goal by their full back, Chris Lawler, sent us down in devastating fashion. While Liverpool spent the next two decades dominating English football and conquering Europe, Sunderland languished for most of this time in the Second Division with the odd highlight of promotion and cup success. When the two sides met it was normally Liverpool who came out on top. After we won promotion in 1980 the Reds hammered us 4-2 at

Barry Venison in Liverpool colours at Roker Park behind Peter Beardsley.

OLD BOYS

Kennedy, Doig, Gayle ...

Sunderland-born Alan Kennedy had a roundabout journey before arriving at his hometown club. As a teenager he broke into the Newcastle United team and played in the 1974 FA Cup Final against Liverpool. The Merseyside club paid £330,000 for the services of the young full back in 1978. Seven years and over 250 League appearances later, he signed for Sunderland for a £100,000 fee. The highlight of his career came in 1981 when he scored the winning goal in the European Cup Final against Real Madrid. Kennedy won his first England cap nine years after being selected to play for his country. Don Revie picked him to play but he

Alan Kennedy

had to drop out because of injury. He had to wait almost a decade before Bobby Robson chose him for the international against Northern Ireland in April 1984. His next cap the following month against Wales was to be his last. Others who have played for both clubs include: David Hannah, Teddy Doig, David Hodgson, Howard Gayle and Paul Stewart.

Roker Park. A friend of mine was so sickened by the performance he left at half time, when the score was 2-0, and missed four goals. Ten years later, again after winning promotion, there was a similar disappointing game, when the two sides met at Roker. Ray Houghton scored the only goal in a typical Liverpool counter attack to kill off the home side – how many times have you seen Liverpool do that? There was also the time when we played them in the FA Cup in the early 1980s. With Roker Park packed, the home crowd were willing Sunderland on until Kenny Dalglish scored one of the greatest goals I've seen. With his back to goal he quickly turned and sent the ball into the back of the net with our defence and goalkeeper almost motionless. It was pure class. A similar goal is often shown on TV but this one was even better.

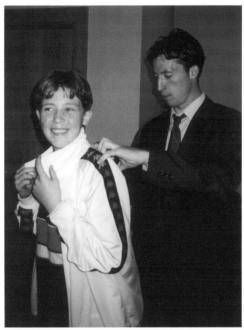

Craig Stewart gets the autograph of Liverpool and England striker Robbie Fowler after the League Centenary match in 1999.

One of the few times we have got the better of Liverpool was when we played them at the end of 1980-81 season when we needed a victory at Anfield to secure First Division status. No-one gave us a chance but a goal by Stan Cummins saw that there was no repeat of the disappointment of ten years before. Perhaps we were lucky that day. Liverpool were due to play in the Final of the European Cup and rested a few players and the fact that their manager, Bob Paisley, was a Sunderland supporter probably helped as well. But, at least for one game, the Liverpool curse was lifted.

Ronnie McGuire

Top of the World

On 21st November 1973 a crowd of 36,208 turned out on a Wednesday afternoon to see Liverpool in a League Cup tie at Roker Park. The goalscorers in a 2-0 Liverpool victory have gone on to two of the top management jobs in the world – Kevin Keegan as England coach and John Toshack at Real Madrid.

Manchester United

Manchester United started life as Newton Heath and their first League encounters with Sunderland came in 1893. At the time Sunderland were reigning League champions while Newton Heath had just been promoted from the Alliance. When the sides met on 4th March 1893 Sunderland were lying top and Newton Heath were bottom. Centre forward Johnny Campbell got two of the goals in a comfortable 5-0 Sunderland victory in Manchester.

By the time of the return fixture a month later Sunderland were already crowned champions. Ironically it was Newton Heath's victory over closest rivals Preston North End that ensured Sunderland retained the title. Sunderland showed their thanks by hammering Newton Heath 6-0 at Newcastle Road on 4th April 1893. The *Echo* reported: 'The ball was cleared, but sent across again by Wilson to Hannah, and the latter coming up, found his head in the way, and used it to pop on the first goal for Sunderland inside ten minutes from the start.' Further goals from Campbell (2), Miller (2) and Wilson completed a convincing double over a club that would one day become Champions of Europe.

Peter Davenport in action against his former club Manchester United in 1990.

OLD BOYS

Turner, Nicholl, Holton ...

During the 1984-85 League (Milk) Cup run Chris Turner was in outstanding form in the Sunderland goal. The former Sheffield Wednesday 'keeper played a major part in getting Sunderland to Wembley. A few months after the Final he moved to Manchester United for a £275,000 fee. Chris is now back in the North East as manager of Hartlepool. After taking over with the threat of going out of the League looming, the former Sunderland and Manchester United man got some brilliant performances out of his men to ensure Hartlepool's survival.

Chris Turner

Northern Ireland regular Jimmy Nicholl made over 200 League and Cup appearances for Manchester United. In the early 1980s he divided his time between Sunderland and Toronto in Canada. Others who have played for both clubs include: Ernie Taylor, Jim Holton, Alan Foggon and Colin Waldron and Terry Cooke.

The Greatest

We have enjoyed some great games over the years with Manchester United. Perhaps the most famous are those FA Cup ties in the 1960s when Best, Law and Charlton were in the United side. Everyone of a certain age seems to have a story about that game at Roker when the ground was packed to overflowing and the game was end to end action. That was before my time so my personal favourites include the match when Clive Walker scored a hat-trick to bring us back from 2-0 down, the game at Roker when Bryan Robson was sent off and the FA Cup tie in the 1990s when Cantona scored in the final minutes at Old Trafford to earn a replay. But in my opinion the best game was in 1990 when this time it was Sunderland's turn to score a late goal – and what a goal it was. It was only our third game back in the old First Division after we had won promotion when Swindon had been found guilty of making illegal payments. At that time the novelty of being in the top flight hadn't worn off and the visit of Manchester United was eagerly awaited. Alex Ferguson was just beginning to build the side that would soon win every honour in the game but that day Sunderland were the greatest. Gary Owers had put Sunderland in front with a header only for Brian McClair to equalise. With time running out it seemed the game was going to finish as a draw then all of a sudden Gary Bennett went racing forward from defence looking unstoppable. He seemed to come from nowhere and there wasn't many Sunderland players up to support him. But they were not needed as he chipped the ball over Gary Pallister and slotted it home to win the game for Sunderland. I had never seen a goal like it.

Matthew Johnson

Mark Proctor and Gordon Strachan at Roker Park in the mid 1980s.

Middlesbrough

Benny The Ball

At 5ft 4ins Benny Yorston was one of the smallest centre forwards to turn out for Sunderland. After signing from Aberdeen in January 1932 he made an immediate impact – scoring 7 goals in his first 5 games. Despite a scoring rate of a goal every two games he was transferred to Middlesbrough for a £1,250 fee after only two years at Roker. The little Scot became a big hit at Ayresome Park playing alongside England international George Camsell.

B. YORSTON

Gordon Armstrong in action at Middlesbrough alongside Mark Proctor formerly of Sunderland.

OLD BOYS

Davenport, Bolton, Common …

After making his name at Nottingham Forest under the guidance of Brian Clough, Peter Davenport made a big money move to Manchester United in 1986. A less than happy stay at Old Trafford came to an end when the striker was transferred to Middlesbrough. The highlight of the England international's Roker career was to play in the 1992 FA Cup Final against Liverpool. In the same season he scored a cracking goal against Boro at Roker Park.

Peter Davenport

   Roker legend Joe Bolton moved to Teesside in 1981 for a £200,000 fee and made 59 appearances for Middlesbrough. After replacing Cup Final left back Ron Guthrie, Joe became a regular in the side for the rest of the decade, starting 264 League matches for Sunderland. Joe ended his playing career at Sheffield United. Others who have played for both clubs include: William Agnew, Alf Common, Jackie Mordue, Tommy Urwin, Johnny Sphuler, Benny Yorston, Brian Clough, Stan Anderson, Geoff Butler, Dickie Rooks, George Kinnell, Alan Foggon, David Hodgson, Stan Cummins, Mark Proctor and John Kay (on loan during his Wimbledon days).

Battling Draw

Sunderland's visit to the Riverside Stadium on 6th November 1999 produced a magnificent battling display. After Chris Makin's dismissal for a second yellow card on the half hour, Sunderland had their backs to the wall. At one point when Steve Bould had to go off to have a head wound stitched and Kevin Phillips was down injured – Sunderland were down to 8 men.

With *Sunderland 'Til I Die* echoing around the ground from the Red and White travelling army the rearguard action held out until the 75th minute. Colombian striker Hamilton Ricard bent a curling shot past Tommy Sorenson to break the deadlock.

Immediately after the goal Peter Reid went all out for an equaliser by bringing on Michael Reddy for Michael Gray. Within minutes Niall Quinn was pushed in the back by Phil Stamp for a penalty. The spot kick from Kevin Phillips was brilliantly saved by Schwarzer but young Reddy followed in to score. Sunderland then hung on to the final whistle to earn a 1-1 draw.

The whole nature of the game might have been different if the referee or his assistants had seen an incident early in the match. Television later showed Brian Deane should have been sent off for elbowing Paul Butler in the throat.

A record crowd of 34,793 at the Riverside watched this hard fought Tees-Wear derby. Sunderland extended their unbeaten run in the Premier to 10 games and showed their third place spot in the League was no flash in the pan.

A Visit to The Riverside

A friend of mine is a Middlesbrough fan and invited me to a game at The Riverside. I was very impressed by their new ground and it was a big improvement on Ayresome Park. It was during the last season we were at Roker Park and our new stadium was being built. My Middlesbrough friend told me once we make the move away from Roker we would never look back. At the time I wasn't sure because I thought I would miss the old ground. But he was proved right and the Stadium of Light is well and truly our new home.

Andrew Clark

Andrew Clark meets Bryan Robson on his visit to the Riverside.

Newcastle United

Red & White Magpie

Such was Stan Seymour's reputation on Tyneside that he was known in the game as 'Mr Newcastle'. However, in an interview in 1963 he recalled:

'In my early days I was a Sunderland supporter. Well do I recall the giants of half a century ago. What wonderful players we had in those far-off days! Boyhood favourites come to mind – Billy Hogg, Charlie Thomson, Charlie Buchan, Jackie Mordue, Frank Cuggy, all at Roker Park, along with that great amateur goalkeeper Dr L.R. Roose.'

Born in Kelloe in County Durham, Seymour, despite an offer of a trial from his boyhood favourites, eventually made his name with arch rivals Newcastle via Bradford City and Greenock Morton.

Prince Albert

A. McINROY

Sunderland signed Albert McInroy from Leyland in 1923 for the sum of £100. The goalkeeper received £10 signing-on fee and thought he was rich! His performances for Sunderland earned him an England cap. After six years at Roker the popular 'keeper was transferred to Newcastle United for a £2,750 fee. In 1932 Albert was a member of United's FA Cup-winning team.

OLD BOYS

Given, Broadis, Moncur ...

When Shay Given arrived at Roker Park from Blackburn Rovers on loan in 1996 he was a virtual unknown. By the time his loan period was up his reputation had soared. A string of clean sheets (including 5 in succession) helped Sunderland on their way to promotion. It was a great disappointment to Sunderland fans when the move was not made permanent. And to add insult to injury when he did leave Ewood Park it was for the Black and Whites up the road!

Early in the twentieth century William Agnew became the first player to appear for Sunderland, Newcastle United and Middlesbrough. Just a few of the many others who have played for both Sunderland and Newcastle include: Johnny

Shay Given

Campbell, John Auld, Andy McCombie, Tommy Urwin, Albert McInroy, Joe Devine, Len Shackleton, Ivor Broadis, Ernie Taylor, Stan Anderson, Dave Elliott, Colin Suggett, Ron Guthrie, David Young, Ray Ellison, Tommy Gibb, Bob Moncur, Alan Brown, Steve Hardwick, Alan Kennedy, Jeff Clarke, Barry Venison, Paul Bracewell, Chris Waddle and Lee Clark.

Newcastle supporters stage a pitch invasion during the Play-off game with Sunderland at St James' in 1990.

Newcastle United's Barry Venison in action against his former team at Roker Park in 1992.

Sheffield Wednesday

Unforgettable

Ian Porterfield's Cup Final goal has ensured his place as a Sunderland legend for all time. After his transfer from Raith Rovers in 1967 the stylish midfielder went on to play over 250 League and Cup games for Sunderland. The pinnacle of his career coming at Wembley on 5th May 1973 when he smashed in a right foot shot past David Harvey in the Leeds' goal.

After leaving Sunderland for Hillsborough in July 1977, Ian Porterfield made over one hundred League appearances for Wednesday before moving into football management.

OLD BOYS

Waddle, Woods, Chapman ...

One of the highlights of Chris Waddle's career was scoring in the last League game at Roker Park. His thunderous shot into the Fulwell End goal had fulfilled a lifelong dream. It had taken over twenty years before the England star finally played for the club he had supported as a boy. After leaving Newcastle in 1985, Chris' performances at White Hart Lane brought him to the attention of big spending European clubs. Chris became worshipped in France after his £4 million move to Marseille. On his return to England his talents were still sought in the Premier by Sheffield Wednesday. He joined Sunderland in 1997 after a spell with Bradford City.

Chris Waddle

Former Sheffield Wednesday goalkeeper Chris Woods was on Sunderland's books but never made a League or Cup appearance. However, he had the honour of playing in the Farewell to Roker Park game against Liverpool. Others who have played for both clubs include: John Robinson, Brian Usher, Colin Symm, Fred McIver, Wilf Rostron, Terry Curran, Chris Turner, Bob Bolder, Lee Chapman, Rodger Wylde and John Cooke.

Alan Brown

Alan Brown had spells as manager of both Sunderland and Sheffield Wednesday. His appointment in 1957 brought revolutionary ideas to Roker Park. Priority was given to developing a Youth policy that would become second to none. The benefits of this would not be reaped until the mid '60s.

It came as a bombshell when Brown left to take over at Hillsborough after achieving promotion to the First Division in 1964. He took Wednesday to the FA Cup final but after leading 2-0, Everton fought back to snatch the trophy.

Alan Brown returned to take over at Sunderland in 1968 and was in charge when the club were relegated for the second time in their history.

Right: The programme for Sunderland's visit to Hillsborough on 13th February 1965. This was the first time the clubs had met

since Alan Brown had left Sunderland for Wednesday. Harry Hood latched on to a long clearance from Sandy McLaughlan but his scorching left foot drive was turned over by Ron Springett. George Herd also went close to opening the scoring, his shot going inches wide. Outside right Alan Finney put Wednesday ahead and then Peter Eustace (later Sunderland coach) sealed victory for the home side. Playing centre forward for Wednesday that day was John Hickton. Converted from full back, Hickton, later had a long career with Middlesbrough.

Easy

Every time I see Mark Bright on *Football Focus* or other TV programmes I always think of that game at Hillsborough when Sheffield Wednesday beat us in the FA Cup in 1993. With the game at 0-0 and only a few minutes left I was already thinking about the replay back at Roker Park. Then that cross came over and the immortal words, 'It's an easy one for Norman' were heard. Next thing we know, Norman's dropped the ball and Mark Bright has knocked it in. What a sickener! It's a shame that Tony Norman will always be remembered for that costly error because I thought he was a good goalkeeper. At the end of the match Terry Butcher came over to the Sunderland supporters to lead us in some singing and lift our spirits. It did for few minutes – then it was a depressing journey home.

Billy Swan

Southampton

The Southampton goal comes under pressure at Roker Park.

OLD BOYS

Venison, Watson, Agboola ...

Now a well known face on television, Barry Venison started his career at Sunderland. At the age of twenty he skippered Sunderland in the League (Milk) Cup Final against Norwich City at Wembley in 1985. The following year he was transferred to Liverpool and went on to win League championship and FA Cup winners' medals at Anfield. After spells with Newcastle and Galatasaray he joined Southampton, before a back injury forced the England international's early retirement from the game.

Sunderland's goalscoring sensation Kevin Phillips started his career at Southampton. He never made the breakthrough into the first team at The Dell, where he was used as a full back. After a spell with non-league Baldock Town he

Barry Venison

joined Watford and then moved on to the Stadium of Light. Others who have played for both clubs include: Jimmy Montgomery, Dave Watson, Frank Worthington and Reuben Agboola.

Sunderland's first tie in the 1937 FA Cup run was the long journey to Southampton. Four hundred die hard supporters travelled to the game on a rail excursion. Raich Carter tore a muscle in the game against Arsenal four days before the tie and failed a late fitness test. Goals from Bobby Gurney, Cyril Hornby and Patsy Gallacher gave Sunderland a 3-2 victory. Scottish inside left Gallacher gave a man of the match performance.

There would be three changes from the team that started the Cup run at Southampton to that which triumphed at Wembley four months later. Raich Carter regained his inside right spot from his goalscoring replacement at The Dell, Hornby. Jimmy Gorman who had just joined the club at the time of the Southampton tie replaced Hall at right back who in turn took over Collin's left back position at Wembley. The great Scottish international winger Jimmy Connor was injured in the next Cup tie against Luton Town and was replaced by Eddie Burbanks for the Cup triumph against Preston North End.

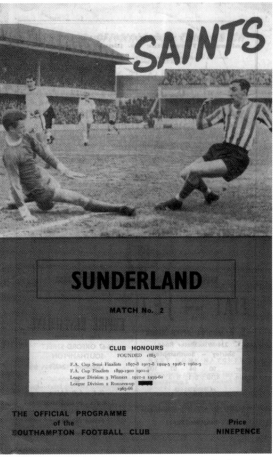

A Southampton programme for Sunderland's long journey south.

Reuben, Reuben

Southampton's Reuben Agboola made the long trip north to join Sunderland in 1985. He was soon followed by his former boss at The Dell, Lawrie McMenemy. Reuben's stay at Roker certainly did not lack incident: the side was twice relegated from the First Division, relegated from the Second Division, promoted from the Third Division and promoted from the Second Division. He left the club early in the season we reached the FA Cup Final.

Tottenham Hotspur

Campbell's Class

When Sunderland played Tottenham in the FA Cup in 1995 it was a chance to see one of the best players in the world – Jurgen Klinsmann. The game was live on television and afterwards I found out that one of the cameras was just behind me and my friends in the Clock Stand. So every time that camera was used you could see the backs of our heads. After Gary Bennett was sent off for hand ball there was a sense of inevitability that we would get beat. I thought their best player was Sol Campbell. He was just starting his career then and it was before he was established in the England side. Sunderland never got a sniff in front of the Spurs' goal. We played Craig Russell and Martin Smith up front and in every challenge they were just bouncing off Campbell.

Matthew Johnson

England star Sol Campbell challenges Craig Russell. When Campbell played at the Stadium of Light in October 1999 he could not contain the Quinn/Phillips partnership – Sunderland running out 2-1 winners.

OLD BOYS

Stewart, Seed, Waddle ...

Sunderland and Tottenham were just two of the clubs Paul Stewart had on his long football travels. The highlight of his career must have been scoring against Nottingham Forest at Wembley in the 1991 to help win the FA Cup. One of the low points must have been missing a header in front of goal at Wimbledon which might have kept Sunderland in the Premiership.

Jimmy Seed was still recovering from the effects of being gassed in the First World War when he turned out for Sunderland in the Victory League in 1919. Sunderland did not sign him on medical grounds but Spurs did and he went on to become an England international. Bobby Mimms and Chris Waddle are two other players who have appeared for both clubs.

Paul Stewart

Echo
SUNDERLAND

Football Echo
EDITION

No. 30.218 (95th YEAR)   SUNDERLAND ECHO AND SHIPPING GAZETTE, SATURDAY, NOVEMBER 16, 1968   FIVEPENCE

GREAVES'S SNAP GOALS SUBDUE SUNDERLAND

TODAY'S FOOTBALL RESULTS

He goes poaching for Spurs and bags four

TOTTENHAM HOTSPUR 5   SUNDERLAND - - - - 1
SUNDERLAND were happy to rely upon the side which
played against Manchester Utd. last week for their visit to

DIVISION 1	F.A. CUP: 1st Round	
Burnley ... 1 Wolves ... 1	Altrincham 0 Crewe Alex. 1	Hartlepools 1 Rotherham 1
Chelsea ... 2 South'mpt'n 3	Bangor C... 2 Morecambe 3	Hereford ... 0 Torquay ... 0
Coventry v. Leeds	Barnet ... 1 Brentwood 1	Leytonstone 0 Walsall ... 1
Everton ... 4 Q.P.R. ... 0	Barnsley v. Rochdale	Luton T ... 6 Ware ... 1
Man. Utd. 0 Ipswich ... 0	Bilston ... 1 Halifax ... 3	Macclesf'ld 1 Lincoln C... 3
		Mansfield 4 Tow Law ... 1

The *Football Echo* of 16th November 1968. Centre half Mike England partnered Greaves up front and scored Spurs' other goal. Billy Hughes got Sunderland's consolation goal.

Brief Encounter

I picked up a copy of Jimmy Greaves' book *This One's On Me* and looked in the index for any mention of Sunderland. There was only one entry listed. I turned to page 120 to find:

'Jimmy Greaves snatched four goals in this 5-1 slamming of Sunderland. How much longer can England afford to ignore the claims of Britain's top hot-shot.'

Tommy Taylor

Three Spurs supporters enjoyed the hospitality of the Howard Arms in Roker Avenue before the game in October 1999.

Watford

It Could Have Been Worse

The 25th September 1982 was a black day in Sunderland's encounters with Watford – we went down to a 8-0 defeat at Vicarage Road. Goals from Blissett (4), Callaghan (2) and Jenkins (2) helped Graham Taylor's men inflict a record-equalling defeat on the Wearsiders. It could have been worse – Watford hit the woodwork on another 4 occasions.

After the defeat Sunderland manager Alan Durban said: 'It was not a day of disaster as no player broke a leg, no one was sent off and the fans did not run riot in the town … I only hope that we have not done too much damage with our fans as they were magnificent throughout the game and I really felt sorry for them.'

Sunderland bounced back the following week with a 4-1 win against Norwich City at Roker.

Sunderland boss Alan Durban was philosophical about the 8-0 defeat at Vicarage Road.

OLD BOYS

Phillips, Chamberlain, Rostron …

What has happened to Kevin Phillips since his £650,000 transfer from Watford in the summer of '97 reads like a fairytale. In his first season he broke the club's post-war scoring record and followed up with 23 goals in 26 League games last season. An England debut against Hungary in April 1999 was the icing on the cake for the little striker.

Kevin Phillips

Another fairytale ending happened to a man making the opposite journey. When Alec Chamberlain left Sunderland for Second Division Watford in 1997, thoughts of playing in the Premiership must have been a far off dream. Yet two promotions later he is in the top flight. The former Sunderland 'keeper played a huge part in helping Watford join the elite of English football. Others who have played for both clubs include: Ray Train, Mick Henderson, Wilf Rostron and Colin West.

G Men – Gates and Gabbiadini in the thick of the action against Watford in the 1989-90 season.

Watford Away

I went to Vicarage Road during the 1998-99 season. Sunderland ended up getting beat 2-1. The strangest thing about that game was the way in which the Watford fans celebrated their goals. They took a 1-0 lead and, suddenly, the PA burst into life with the opening bars of 'Papa's Got A Brand New Bag'. Within seconds, the Watford fans were on their feet, swaying and throwing their arms around in a mad dance! Moments later the Sunderland fans joined in – even though we'd just conceded a goal!

We equalised later that half – no music this time. In the second half, we played pretty poorly, and, early on, Watford got a second goal. This time, the Sunderland fans needed no prompt to get on their feet, and were up doing the mad dance themselves to '… Brand New Bag'. It was weird – we weren't celebrating, just dancing for the sake of it. Maybe we were mimicking the Watford fans – I'm still not sure. Strange. Very strange.

Neil Henderson

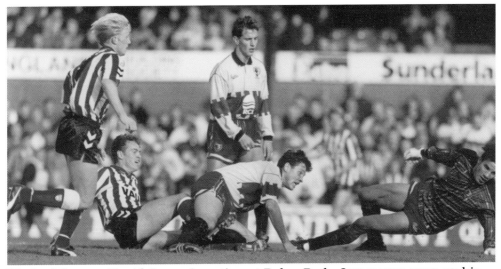

Watford 'keeper David James in action at Roker Park. James was soon on his way to Liverpool in a big money move.

West Ham United

I first saw Kieron Brady play in a youth match at the Charlie Hurley Centre and even then I thought I was witnessing a future star. He was by far the best player on the pitch. The youth games used to get a good crowd in those days and many went to see the talents of young Kieron. I remember one incident very clearly. I was standing by the touch line on a very muddy pitch. The ball came near to where I was standing and Brady ran over towards it. The ground was so muddy I had trouble even walking without slipping but the young Irishman had no such trouble staying on his feet. He glided over to collect the ball and with perfect balance beat two players before putting in a superb cross. I though this player will make it.

Not long afterwards Kieron got his chance in the first team. He really made his mark towards the end of the 1989-90 season when Sunderland won promotion. He came into the side in the March when Sunderland were languishing outside the

Gordon Armstrong and Liam Brady compete for the ball in the West Ham match at Roker Park in 1989-90 season.

OLD BOYS

Robson, McGiven, Swindlehurst ...

There must be something about Bryan Robson that West Ham and Sunderland liked because he had two spells with the Hammers and three at Roker. The Sunderland-born striker was one of the best goalscorers in the business – 238 goals in 585 League games. Today, Bryan is part of Peter Reid's coaching staff at the Stadium of Light.

Bryan Robson

Injury plagued Mick McGiven's career at both Roker and Upton Park. The hard tackling midfielder had to come back from breaking his leg three times. He made over 100 appearances for Sunderland but missed out on the FA Cup Final having played in an early round. Mick moved on to West Ham at the end of 1973 and was only in his mid-twenties when he was forced to give up playing. He then moved on to the Hammers' coaching staff. Others who have played for both clubs include: William Moore, Harry Hooper, Mick McGiven, Keith Coleman, Bryan Robson and David Swindlehurst.

play-off positions and promotion seemed out of our reach. But Brady added that little spark that was needed and we started to put a good run together. I personally believe that Brady was one of the most influential players that season but he never got the recognition he deserved. His most memorable game was against West Ham when he was up against another Brady and Irishman – Liam. But there was only one Brady worth talking about that day and Kieron was the man. He scored one goal – a brilliant overhead kick – and was at the heart of all of Sunderland's play. Sunderland won 4-3 and Kieron was declared a new Roker hero by the crowd. It's such a shame that his potential was never fulfilled. But any supporter who saw Brady play that day will always remember him.

Stephen Morrissey

Kieron Brady takes on a West Ham defender at Roker Park in 1990.

The young Irishman celebrates a goal at the Roker End.

Wimbledon

Not Football

Wimbledon's first ever visit to Roker Park in 1985 was a game I'll never forget. The ball seemed to be up in the air for most of the 90 minutes. Wimbledon never attempted to play any football and their tactics prevented Sunderland from playing. Although Sunderland won the game 2-1 with both goals coming from Dave Swindlehurst, the match was one of the worst I have ever seen. The Dons' manager Dave Bassett's system was to keep pumping high balls into the Sunderland penalty area and hope a goal would come from it. Wimbledon 'keeper Dave Beasant was one of the main sources of supply for the big hoof up field. Any free kick in the Dons' half was taken by the big 'keeper with his ten team-mates waiting for it in the box.

   Wimbledon striker Alan Cork was sent off in the 80th minute for retaliation but Sunderland were already 2-0 up at the time. It was the visitors who then scored two minutes later. Sunderland hung on to take full points in a dreadful match. There was some correspondence in the local press suggesting Sunderland should follow similar tactics because it produced results. Thankfully they did not because I would have given up going to Roker Park. It just wasn't football.

Tommy Taylor

OLD BOYS

Kay, Harford, Entwistle ...

After starting his League career with Arsenal, John Kay moved across London to join Wimbledon in 1984. The hard tackling full back made 63 League appearances with Wimbledon before being snapped up by Sunderland. Like today with Chris Makin, the Sunderland crowd used to will on Kay to shoot and open his goal account. His wholehearted performances made him a big favourite with Roker supporters. A broken leg sustained in a game against Birmingham City in October 1993 was to signal the end of his days at Sunderland.

   Sunderland-born Mick Harford spent a short period with his hometown club in the mid '90s and then ended his career at Wimbledon where he is now part of the coaching staff.

Another player to have turned out for both clubs is Wayne Entwistle. The fact that Wimbledon only entered the Football League in the 1977-78 season helps explain why so few players have appeared for both clubs.

John Kay

Down At Plough Lane

I've been to some disastrous away games but I think the worst was against Wimbledon in the FA Cup in the 1980s. It was when Lawrie McMenemy was the manager and even for those dark days it was terrible. It was the first time I had been to Plough Lane and it was in such a state you can see why Wimbledon decided to ground share rather than play there. One stand in the corner seemed to be just a few garden sheds knocked together. The game itself was fitting to its surroundings. This was about the time when the 'Crazy Gang' were making a name for themselves but no-one that day would think they would go on to such success. Sunderland went into a surprise lead and I started looking forward to the next round and possibly a little cup run to lift the gloom that seemed to exist at Roker Park in those days – fatal mistake! Wimbledon – the team who never gives up – came back to equalise. Now I was thinking, well, at least we can get a draw, take them back to Roker and beat them in the replay. Then disaster occurred with a ridiculous goal in the final minutes. A Wimbledon player was running through with plenty of Sunderland defenders behind the ball. There seemed to be no danger until Gary Bennett and Mark Proctor ran into each other, both fell to the ground and their striker strolled through to score. Once again defeat snatched from the jaws of victory. I walked away thinking how could a club with the tradition of Sunderland be defeated by such a lowly club. It must be a fluke I thought. Wimbledon will never beat us again in an important game. How wrong I was.

Matthew Johnson

Mick Harford during his brief stay with his hometown club.

No Blame

One of the worst things about the defeat at the hands of Wimbledon which relegated us from the Premiership was the long journey home. Car and coach loads of Coventry City supporters were laughing at us as they returned from White Hart Lane having escaped relegation again.

The strange thing is that I don't blame Wimbledon for sending us down but Coventry's day will come.

Ray Wilson

Phillips and Quinn have proved a deadly partnership in the Premier League.

Back Where We Belong

Now Sunderland is back in the Premiership you realise what we have been missing when you play in the Football League. It is not only the football which is second class when you drop out of the Premier. The media coverage revolves around the top clubs which Sunderland are now back with. It's great to see The Lads on *Match of the Day*, Sky television or read about them in the national newspapers and football magazines. With so much attention our players are becoming household names. There will be football fans all around the country following our fortunes – perhaps a few will be converted to support Sunderland for life.

Stephen Morrissey

Play Your Cards Right

Because of its close proximity to the Stadium of Light, the Companions Club is a popular watering hole for supporters. After the first home match of the 1999-2000 season a huge roar could be heard in the club. The large TV screen showed Newcastle United bottom of the Premier League. Then the clubs above them were revealed one by one: 19th Watford, 18th Coventry City, 17th Sheffield Wednesday ... The chant went up 'Higher, Higher' (like Bruce Forsyth's *Play Your Cards Right*). 16th Leicester City, 15th Derby County, 14th Leeds United ... 'Higher, Higher'. 13th Manchester United, 12th Everton and then 11th Sunderland. We were only kept out of 2nd place by goal difference.

ON TOUR WITH THE LADS

Supporters outside Sunderland railway station setting off for the first game of the 1976-77 season at Stoke.

Lucky Strips

When a new set of strips was provided for 1937 FA Cup Final side, trainer Andy Reid was not happy. He thought the kit Sunderland had worn in the rounds leading up to the Final was lucky. A compromise was reached by having the badge from the new shirts transferred to the old.

Left: The programme for the Sunderland v Preston North End Cup Final.

Right: Action from Sunderland's trip to White Hart Lane in March 1958. Sunderland players: right to left: Colin Grainger, Don Revie and Don Kichenbrand. A goal from England international Revie was sufficient to secure Sunderland both points. The game was notable because it was one of only three away victories achieved all season. This helped seal relegation to the Second Division. Massive support both home and away could not save the club losing their status in the top flight for the first time.

Away Days With Aubrey

In the 1970s and '80s we used to travel all over the country following Sunderland. We used to go on coaches run by Aubrey Stores from Red House Club. Aubrey is a real character and would get the coach driver to pull up right outside grounds to drop us off. One day we were heading for Stamford Bridge and we ended up outside Craven Cottage wondering why there was nobody about. After matches we always ended up back at a Leicester Club where we had some great nights.

Ray Redman

Above and left: Supporting Sunderland seventies style.

Unbelievable

I was at Highbury for the FA Cup tie in 1997. I was with a friend from the Isle of Man who could not believe the noise the Sunderland supporters made. He had never witnessed supporters keep up such vocal support throughout the whole game. It frightened him.

Michael McDonagh

Turf Moor Memories

I travelled to Burnley for the last away game of the 1994-95 season. We drew the match 1-1 with a goal from Martin Smith. The game was nothing to write home about but something that happened after the match has always stuck in my mind. Leaving Turf Moor we were in a coach that formed a seemingly endless convoy. I still recall the look of amazement on the face of a woman at a house window. She and a young child waved at the Sunderland fans as they left for home. Would they ever see such visiting support in their lifetime again? Let's hope if it's against Sunderland it's because Burnley make it to the Premier!

Susan Wilkinson

A view from the back of the stands at Turf Moor during the last away match of the 1994-95 season.

Christmas Day In Foggy Leeds

At one time League matches used to be played on Christmas Day. My dad (Stan Farrer) travelled to Leeds to watch a Festive game. His brother Wilf, worked on the railways and got cheap train tickets for the trip. They arrived at Leeds only to find the match called off because of fog. They could not return until the time on the tickets and so spent Christmas Day looking in the shop windows of Leeds. A Christmas to remember for the wrong reasons.

Peter Farrer

Burnley Blues

The first away match I went to was the FA Cup match at Burnley in 1979. It was postponed about eight times, my dad was going mad because each time I was taking time off school to go.

Phil Reynolds

Following The Lads

Scot Stewart (left) on tour with The Lads.

When Sunderland were in the Premier League in 1996-97 season we travelled all over the country to see them. We sat down and calculated we had spent a fortune on that one season. Since the wife found out what I had been spending following The Lads she has made sure I take her on holiday two or three times a year. Even then the fixture list comes between us. When we booked up a fortnight in Tenerife I thought I could fit it in between the Coventry City game on 29th August 1999 and Leicester City on 11th September but I miscalculated and missed the Leicester match.

Scot Stewart

Cambridge Away

Years ago, I went to Cambridge's Abbey Stadium to watch The Lads. I can't remember the year or the occasion, but what I can remember is that Cambridge's ground is possibly the least aptly named in the country: 'Stadium?' – I think not! I don't remember the score or what the game was like but I do recall two things: Dion Dublin was guest of honour for the day (having recently joined Man United from Cambridge), and there was a 'rookie policewoman' standing on the turf right in front of us. She looked really young - probably just out of her teens. At one point in the first half, somebody in the crowd swore, and another fan immediately shouted, 'Ow, watch your language, man, there's young 'uns on the pitch!' I think the young copper must have heard this because she blushed really badly. This was just a red rag to a bull and the Sunderland fans spent the next ten minutes singing 'Policewoman, policewoman, policewoman, policewoman, po-lice-wo-man!' She seemed very very embarrassed, but eventually took the whole thing in the good-nature it was intended, and took a bow! Her boss even came across to applaud the fans!

Neil Henderson

Trafalgar Square Party

I was down London for the Crystal Palace match in April 1999 and ended up in Trafalgar Square on the night. Loads of Sunderland supporters gathered there to celebrate, although promotion was not quite guaranteed. Metro FM's Gilly and Gatsey had bottled out of coming. Then Gatsey appeared on one of the lions. He shouted 'I'm Here, Anyone not in the fountain isn't a Sunderland supporter.' There was a mass rush for the fountain. There were thousands around the Trafalgar Square looking on. It was unbelievable.

Darren Bland

Supporters outside The Torch public house at the top of Wembley Way before the 1998 Play-off Final. Included are: Andy Colborn and the Stewart Clan – Gorman, Craig, Scot and Jamie.

Another Heartbreaker

The first away match I saw Sunderland play was the last match of the 1961-62 season against Swansea. I was stationed in Germany at the time and we had to fly over for the game. Sunderland had to win to clinch promotion and as we had beaten Swansea 7-2 at Roker Park earlier in the season we thought we could do it. But we could only manage a 1-1 draw and lost out on promotion. I remember a header from Charlie Hurley that was going in the top corner of the goal when the Swansea 'keeper appeared from nowhere to tip the ball away.

Matty Morrison

Anfield Memories

The first away game I went to was the FA Cup tie against Liverpool in 1961. I organised the coach trip with my mate John Avery but as we were both only sixteen we booked the coach in John's dad's name. It was a great day out with Sunderland winning 2-0. Harry Hooper and Ian Lawther got the goals, both going over the head of the little Liverpool 'keeper Slater. Len Ashurst had one of his best games for Sunderland marking the dangerous Alan A'Court out of the game.

On the coach afterwards I remember hearing on the radio that Manchester City's tie against Luton had been abandoned with City leading 6-2. Denis Law had scored all six goals for City. When the match was replayed a few days later Law was again on the scoresheet but ended up on the losing side.

Michael Bute

Buxton Out!

During Mick Buxton's last season in charge, I went down to Vicarage Road to see Sunderland play Watford. We'd been playing really badly in recent weeks and finding it hard to score. Watford, on the other hand, had gone nine games without conceding a goal – a club record at the time.

Moments after kick-off, a Sunderland supporter and his young son (who must have been about eight-years-old) stood up and started singing, 'We want Buxton out, we want Buxton out!' Nobody was paying any attention to them, but they carried on their solo protest regardless. Half an hour or so into the game, Sunderland scored. All the Sunderland fans started celebrating like mad and chants of 'What's it like to see a goal?' were directed at The Hornets' fans. Then, just when everything had calmed down, and everyone had retaken their seats, the bloke and his son stood up again. This time they chanted, 'We STILL want Buxton out, we STILL want Buxton out!' This seemed hilarious in the context of Sunderland winning, and fans around them were laughing out loud. But still they carried on. Now that's dedication to the cause!

Neil Henderson

Eighty And Counting

I've been to 80 League grounds to watch Sunderland. The visit to West Ham in October 1999 meant I have been to all the clubs in the Premier League.

Scot Stewart

Right: A young Sunderland supporter at Blackburn in 1999.

The Great Escape, Almost

I was down Leeds for the Boxing Day match in 1986. After the game, which Sunderland drew, we found out our coach had broken down and we would have to make our own way home. Vaux trips always had the worst coaches and this one was so old I'm surprised it made it to Leeds in the first place.

We went around to the players entrance and explained what had happened to the Sunderland party about to leave for home. Barry Batey was all for us joining them on the coach but Lawrie McMenemy would have none of it. When no-one was looking me and my mate 'Lamma' sneaked in the side where the luggage was kept. It was like a something from *The Great Escape* and we were all set for the journey home. But someone had forget to put their case in. The driver got the shock of his life when he opened the door and found us in there. Our escape plan to get back to Sunderland was rumbled by one of the 'guards'.

Richie Cooney

The Blackburn programme for Sunderland's first season back in Division One in 1964-65 season. Earlier in the season a crowd of over 40,000 saw a Nicky Sharkey goal secure full points for Sunderland. For the return at Ewood Park barely 10,000 saw Sunderland go down to the odd goal in five. At this time Rovers had stars like Bryan Douglas, Mike England and Ronnie Clayton but the following season they were relegated. They were then in the football wilderness until rescued by Jack Walker's millions.

Stars of the Big Screen

In recent years I have made the trip west to Blackburn. The condition of Ewood Park is a big improvement on the old days when it was a fairly poor stadium. Jack Walker's millions have gone on redevelopment both on and off the pitch. I thought it was interesting that in one corner they have a big screen – I think they call them 'jumbotrons'. Just before kick off you could see the teams line up in the tunnel ready to make their entrance.

Ronnie McGuire

Below: An unusual view of the Sunderland team coming out for the FA Cup tie at Blackburn. Ewood Park's state of the art 'jumbotron'.

ODDS AND ENDS

I never touched a drop Guv'nor – Paul Ince looking the worse for wear but only drinking Lucozade. Sandwiched between his former Liverpool team-mate Robbie Fowler is Craig Stewart. The occasion was the League Centenary match at the Stadium of Light in May 1999.

Clem Stephenson

In 1921 it appeared Sunderland were all set to sign Clem Stephenson from Aston Villa. New Daleval-born Stephenson was suspended by Villa for a fortnight for failing to arrive in time for a game at Bolton. He was living outside Newcastle at the time and after the incident Villa demanded all their players should live in Birmingham. Stephenson was not happy and a move back to the North East appeared on the cards when Huddersfield stepped in to sign him.

Stephenson was a brilliant inside forward and a great strategist. A former chairman of Huddersfield recalled how Herbert Chapman on his appointment as manager said the young players needed a 'general' to lead them on the field. That man was Clem Stephenson.

Instead of gracing Roker Park, Stephenson went on to help Huddersfield to a hat-trick of League titles between 1924 and 1926. He also won an FA Cup winners' medal to go with two he gained with Villa.

Could Stephenson have inspired Sunderland to the same success? While Stephenson played a big part in Huddersfield's fortunes a large part of the credit must go to

Clem Stephenson

manager Herbert Chapman. After winning the first two championships and laying the foundation for the third, Chapman left to take over at Arsenal. He repeated his winning ways at Highbury – claiming the FA Cup in 1930 and the League the following year. Arsenal then won three successive championships between 1933 and 1935 (Chapman died halfway through the second triumph).

Chapman's first signing at Arsenal was Sunderland's Charlie Buchan. The former Roker favourite was an instant success at Highbury and fulfilled the same tactical role as Stephenson had done for him at Huddersfield.

I Had A Dream

When Sunderland met Aston Villa in the 1913 FA Cup Final they had a strange encounter with Clem Stephenson. Peter Morris in his book *Aston Villa* revealed what happened: 'After about ten minutes when the ball had gone outside and was being retrieved for a throw-in, there was a remarkable conversation between Clem Stephenson and Charles Buchan which went something like this:

Stephenson: "We shall beat you today, Charlie."

Buchan: "What do you mean – beat us?"

Stephenson: "I dreamed it last night and I saw Tommy Barber head the winning goal too. You wait and see."

Buchan: "Get away with you!"

Only minutes before full time Barber duly headed Villa's winner as prophesied by Stephenson.

Roker Park was the venue for not only football occasions. Here a Rosary Crusade at the old ground in the 1950s takes over the pitch and terraces. A large crowd looked on despite the wet conditions.

Gentleman George

George Hardwick's appointment as Sunderland manager in November 1964 came as a big surprise to supporters. In his book *Gentleman George*, George Hardwick recalled how he could not resist the challenge of the Roker Park hot seat when it was offered to him. He was aware that Don Revie and Tommy Docherty had rejected the post before his appointment.

George's football pedigree was second to none: captain of Middlesbrough, England and Great Britain, Oldham Athletic player/manager, Director of Coaching of the Dutch national team and PSV Eindhoven coach/manager.

Despite keeping Sunderland in the First Division in the 1964-65 season he was sacked in the summer of '65.

A lasting legacy of George Hardwick's time at Roker was to give Brian Clough his first coaching job with Sunderland Youths. When George was offered the Hartlepool job he declined but suggested Brian Clough was the man for the Victoria Ground – the rest is history.

Radio Times

The radio commentary team of Guy, Gilly and Gatesy are sadly missed by Sunderland supporters. There was a time, however, when Sunderland were in the forefront of a campaign to end such match commentaries.

At a meeting of the Football League on 2nd June 1951 Sunderland proposed that live radio broadcasts of League games should be banned. The motion was passed but the ban was rescinded a couple of months later at a meeting of Football League clubs.

Left: Eric Gates in his playing days. The Ferryhill-born striker started his career at Ipswich Town in the early '70s. When he joined Sunderland in 1985 he was an England international.

Death Knell of the Rattle

For years the terraces of Roker Park echoed to the sound of rattles. These originally had a number of uses. Corn crakes were used in the countryside to scare birds off crops. In towns and cities wooden rattles were used by nightwatchmen and policemen to summon help in emergencies. Around 1884 local police replaced the rattle with a whistle. Not all policemen in Sunderland welcomed the change – the heavy rattle had doubled up as a good weapon.

Fulham to Italy via Sunderland

After Sunderland AFC Supporters' Association was formed in the mid 1960s we were always on the look out for stock to sell in our shop. Fulham contacted us and asked if we were interested in a batch of corn crakes. When Sunderland played at Craven Cottage in March 1966 we got the driver of one of our coaches to pick them up. They arrived in a big crate smelling of creosote. Considering they had been stored at Fulham since the Second World War they were in remarkable condition. They were each wrapped in grease-proof paper. I roped John Bousfield into giving me a hand to clean and paint them. We spent hours doing this and at one point rattles were hanging up to dry all round the house. Some we painted with red and white stripes for Sunderland supporters. As the World Cup at Roker Park was approaching we also painted some in blue and white to sell to Italian supporters. However, when they arrived they did not want them, they wanted something with World Cup Willie on. Once we attached stickers of the World Cup mascot on them we sold them all. I think we bought the batch of 100 corn crakes from Fulham for £1 each and sold them for £2. No doubt there are still a few scattered in Sunderland households today. As for those that went to Italy I wonder if any find their way to Serie A grounds?

George Forster

The old Supporters' Association shop in Roker Baths Road.

In The League 'Til They Died

Playing in the Premier League is a far cry from the dark days of Division Three, however, supporters of some clubs would welcome even that level of football. Aldershot and Doncaster Rovers were two clubs Sunderland played against in the 1987-88 season who are now no longer in the Football League.

Sunderland have had links with many of the dozens of clubs who have gone out of the League since 1888.

Accrington were one of the twelve original members of the Football league in 1888. When Sunderland entered the League two years later they faced Accrington for the next three seasons. Sunderland got the better of League meetings with the Lancashire club: winning four, drawing two and losing only one game, with a further two victories in FA Cup ties. Accrington left the League in 1893 but a new club appeared in 1921 in the Third Division North as Accrington Stanley. In 1962 they left the League for good.

Sunderland's last ever visit to Aldershot before their demise.

Darwen were another club Sunderland encountered in the early years who are no longer in the League. In 1891-92 season Sunderland beat Darwen 7-0 at home and 7-1 away. The previous season Sunderland had also beat Darwen 2-0 in the FA Cup. In the 1893-94 season, Darwen's last in the First Division, they managed to hold Sunderland to only a 3-0 scoreline home and away. Darwen went out of the League in 1899.

From South Shields To Gateshead

When Sunderland signed Warney Cresswell from South Shields in 1922 for £5,500 he was already an England international. He played against Wales in March 1921 when the Tyneside club were in the Second Division.

Prior to joining the League, South Shields acquired the services of Sunderland and England winger Arthur Bridgett. In the summer of 1912 Bridgett became South Shields player-manager for a £175 transfer fee.

In 1930 the South Shields club moved lock, stock and barrel to Gateshead and remained in the League under this name. Sunderland continued to have connections with the club. During the last war they played Gateshead many times in various wartime competitions.

Arthur Bridgett

George Aitken was transferred from Sunderland to Fourth Division Gateshead in May 1959 for a £1,500 fee. Eight years before Sunderland had signed the Scottish international from Third Lanark (who went out of the Scottish League in 1967). Former Sunderland chief scout, Charlie Ferguson, took over as manager at Gateshead but could not save them going out of the League in 1960.

The *Football Echo's* view of the FA Cup visit of Bradford Park Avenue in 1938. In the build up to the game the Bradford team were reported to have been on a high energy diet of raw eggs and sherry.

Both Accrington and Darwen met Sunderland in their prime. Between 1892 and 1895 Sunderland won the title three times and were runners-up on the other occasion.

The Derbyshire town of Glossop added 'North End' to their name in honour of the famous Preston club. When they were promoted to the First Division in 1899 they became the smallest town (25,000 population) to play in the top division and dropped the 'North End'. Sunderland beat Glossop 2-0 away in October 1899 but were held to a 0-0 draw at Roker Park later in the season. This was to be Glossop's only season in the top flight and they went out of the League at the time of the First World War. However, before they did they provided Sunderland with one of their top goalkeepers. Joe Butler never missed a game for Second Division Glossop for three seasons before joining Sunderland in October 1912. In that season Butler's performances helped Sunderland to the League title and FA Cup Final.

Sunderland played Bradford Park Avenue in the First Division in the last season before the First World War and the first two after. Of the six League meetings Sunderland were ahead by just one win but they beat Park Avenue in two FA Cup matches. In 1910 goals from Low (2) and Bridgett gave Sunderland a comfortable home win. In 1938 a Len Duns goal was enough to give victory before a crowd of 59,326 again at Roker Park. Bradford Park Avenue's most famous player was Len Shackleton, who of course later starred for Sunderland and England. In 1970 Park Avenue were voted out of the League after seeking re-election for the fourth season in succession.

Automatic relegation from the Football League and promotion from the Conference League was introduced in 1986-87. Until then the bottom four clubs in the lowest division used to seek re-election. This system sometimes produced clearly unfair outcomes. In 1960 Gateshead finished third from bottom of the Fourth Division. It was the first time they had to seek re-election since 1937. Oldham, who finished below Gateshead, were seeking re-election for a second time in a row and 4th from bottom Southport were seeking re-election for a third successive year. But it was Gateshead who were voted out of the League in favour of Peterborough. The geographical isolation of the North East was probably responsible for Gateshead's demise.

Ken Chisholm was the leading marksman at Sunderland in the 1954-55 season but a year later he signed for Workington on a free transfer. The Cumbrian club had been admitted to the League in 1951 and lost their place in 1977. Before their League days Bobby Gurney broke his leg at Workington playing for Sunderland Reserves.

Losing Football League status need not mean the end of the world for clubs. Despite automatic relegation the system does allow a route back into the League. After being relegated to the Conference League in 1989 Darlington bounced back after only one season. Former Roker favourite George Mulhall also guided Halifax Town back into the League in the 1997-98 season.

Right: The programme for Sunderland's first ever game outside the top flight. The opponents that day Lincoln City were relegated from the Football League in 1987 but have since regained their League status.

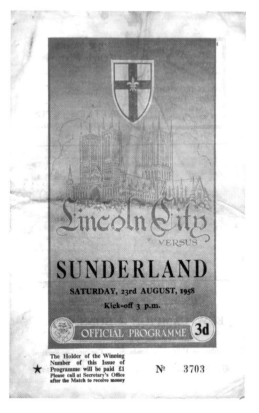

Showing the Flag – Charlotte, Harry and Rebecca Richardson. Nor are these just armchair supporters, all three of these young 'uns have been to matches at the Stadium of Light.